ON DISSENT

America values dissent. It tolerates, encourages, and protects it. But what is this thing we value? That is a question never asked. "Dissent" is treated as a known fact. For all that has been said about dissent – in books, articles, judicial opinions, and popular culture – it is remarkable that no one has devoted much, if any, ink to explaining what dissent is. No one has attempted to sketch its philosophical, linguistic, legal, or cultural meanings or usages. There is a need to develop some clarity about this phenomenon we call dissent, for not every difference of opinion, symbolic gesture, public activity in opposition to government policy, incitement to direct action, revolutionary effort, or political assassination needs be tagged dissent. In essence, we have no conceptual yardstick. It is just that measure of meaning that *On Dissent* offers.

Ronald K. L. Collins is the Harold S. Shefelman Scholar at the University of Washington Law School. Collins was a scholar at the Washington, DC, office of the First Amendment Center, where he wrote and lectured on freedom of expression, and where he is still a Senior Fellow. His journalistic writings on the First Amendment have appeared in *Columbia Journalism Review*, the *New York Times*, and the *Washington Post*, among other publications. He is the book editor of SCOTUSblog. In addition to the books that he has coauthored with David M. Skover, Collins is the editor of *Oliver Wendell Holmes: A Free Speech Chronicle and Reader* (2010) and coauthor, with Sam Chaltain, of *We Must Not Be Afraid to Be Free* (2011). His latest book is *Nuanced Absolutism: Floyd Abrams and the First Amendment* (2013).

David M. Skover is the Fredric C. Tausend Professor of Law at Seattle University School of Law. He teaches, writes, and lectures in the fields of federal constitutional law, federal jurisdiction, mass communications theory, and the First Amendment. Skover graduated from the Woodrow Wilson School of International and Domestic Affairs at Princeton University. He received his law degree from Yale Law School, where he was an editor of the *Yale Law Journal*. Thereafter, he served as a law clerk for Judge Jon O. Newman of the U.S. Court of Appeals for the Second Circuit. In addition to the books that he has coauthored with Ronald K. L. Collins, he is the coauthor, with Pierre Schlag, of *Tactics of Legal Reasoning* (1986).

ON DISSENT

ITS MEANING IN AMERICA

RONALD K. L. COLLINS & DAVID M. SKOVER

CAMBRIDGE UNIVERSITY PRESS
Cambridge, New York, Melbourne, Madrid, Cape Town,
Singapore, São Paulo, Delhi, Mexico City

Cambridge University Press
32 Avenue of the Americas, New York, NY 10013-2473, USA

www.cambridge.org
Information on this title: www.cambridge.org/9780521767194

First published 2013

Printed in the United States of America

A catalog record for this publication is available from the British Library.

Library of Congress Cataloging in Publication Data

Collins, Ronald K. L., author.
On dissent : its meaning in America / Ronald K.L. Collins, University of
Washington, Law School, Seattle, David M. Skover, Seattle University,
School of Law.
pages cm.
Includes bibliographical references and index.
ISBN 978-0-521-76719-4 (hardback)
1. Government, Resistance to – United States   2. Dissenting opinions –
United States.   3. Judicial opinions – United States.   4. Dissenters –
Legal status, laws, etc. – United States.   I. Skover, David M., 1951–
author.   II. Title.
KF4786.C65   2013
322.40973–dc23   2012042745

ISBN 978-0-521-76719-4 Hardback

To the Memory of

THOMAS PAINE

**and to the
Spirit of All Americans
Who Dare to Heed His Creed of Dissent**

CONTENTS

INFORMATIONIS PERSONAE

Much in what follows is grounded in Socratic premises: that thought develops best when it is engaged; that the give-and-take of ideas improves them; and that certainty is humbled by nuance. Our thinking has been tested time and again by the astute observations and challenges of our *Informationis Personae*. We gratefully acknowledge the twenty-two distinguished persons – jurists, legal scholars, philosophers, sociologists, historians, religious studies professors, political theorists, communication theorists, social activists, and even a renowned media personality – who were considerate enough to share their time and thoughts with us in our efforts to examine the parameters of dissent. Such an examination is particularly important when an ontology of a topic such as dissent is rigorously explored for the first time. Moreover, our *Personae* kindly permitted us to draw from our recorded interviews with them (circa 2004–2012) for use throughout the book. In the same Socratic spirit, we encourage our readers to join this dialogic process, if only to sharpen their own minds on the subject matter.

♋ ♌

Randy E. Barnett	Noam Chomsky	Phil Donahue
Todd Gitlin	Steven K. Green	Kent Greenawalt
Sue Curry Jansen	Sut Jhally	Anita K. Krug
Hans A. Linde	Catharine A. MacKinnon	Ralph Nader
Jon O. Newman	Martha C. Nussbaum	Frederick Schauer
Steven H. Shiffrin	Faith Stevelman	Geoffrey R. Stone
Nadine Strossen	Michael Walzer	Cornel West
	Howard Zinn	

PROLOGUE

Dissent. It is a word we all know, and yet do not know.

We use the word with regularity in any variety of contexts. Judges dissent against a court majority. Political activists dissent against the establishment. Religious protesters dissent against orthodoxy. Students dissent against an administration. Newspaper editorialists dissent against politicians. Employees dissent against management. The list goes on.

In these ways and others, America values dissent, or so it seems. We often tolerate, encourage, and protect dissent. It is part of our Madisonian heritage. Some preach it, some practice it, others safeguard it, and still others endure it even when they oppose its message. Dissent is a salient feature of our modern society. It is a cultural and constitutional given.

Over the ages, dissent has been championed for assorted reasons. Dissent, it might be said, promotes self-realization and autonomy. It enables individual self-expression without fear of societal repression. The liberty of self is meaningless if one must always conform to majority will. Freedom for the outsider allows a unique brand of self-identity and self-expression.

Dissent, it might be said, advances religious freedom. When people of faith are permitted to question prevailing beliefs, they stand to redefine the relationship between themselves and their Maker. This spirit of moderation extinguishes the fires of heresy.

Dissent, it might also be said, contributes to the marketplace of ideas. It does this by promoting competition among divergent viewpoints. The hope is that, in the battle of opinions, some form of truth will prevail over falsehood, and the struggle will produce a more enlightened citizenry.

Dissent, it might further be said, enables self-governance by civic participation. Such participation is a two-way street: it is the prerogative to agree or disagree with governmental action. When the governed rule, they must have the right to differ from their governors.

Dissent, it might be said, checks governmental abuses of power. When the whistle-blower exposes governmental corruption or malfeasance, political power then comes under public scrutiny. By raising citizen awareness, dissent might bring about institutional reforms.

Dissent might moreover cultivate a democratic culture of tolerance, where all views are suffered no matter how objectionable they may be. Democracy is diversity, and diversity of views is often born out of dissent. One measure of a thriving democracy is the extent to which it fosters vibrant dissent.

Finally, it might also be said that a culture of dissent secures a safe haven for the outsider. When individuals no longer fear censure simply for being different, they can give public voice to their private views. Thereby, dissenters are afforded a chance to expand the behavioral boundaries of their society.

Whatever the objections to dissent, it is valued for all these reasons and others. But what is it we value? When we speak of dissent, what is it of which we speak? When we converse – in homes, schools, offices, court chambers, legislative arenas, and in public generally – how do we use this word? How is it understood? These and other questions are rarely, if ever, asked.

The word "dissent" is treated as a known. When we use it, we seldom quibble over what we mean or understand it to be. It can be good or bad, safe or dangerous, peaceful or violent, prophetic or blasphemous, laudatory or offensive, legal or illegal. But that "it" is an uncontested constant. "Dissent" does its linguistic work with few decipherable, conceptual traces. In this way, "dissent" is like air – we breathe it without noticing it, and its invisibility belies its importance.

This is a curious – indeed, unfortunate – state of affairs. For if we talk about dissent without giving it any ideational content or without appreciating how we actually use the word, we cannot really know what to value or what to safeguard.

Such mental quantum leaps are certainly not accepted elsewhere. Take the idea of justice, for instance. What is it? That question, recall, was the starting point for Plato's classic, *The Republic*. The query continues into modernity with works such as Elizabeth Wolgast's *The Grammar of Justice*.

What is equality? That concern was the focus of Rousseau's 1755 work, entitled *Second Discourse*. It finds contemporary expression in books such as Thomas Nagel's *Equality and Partiality*.

What is property? That inquiry inspired Pierre Proudhon's seminal 1840 book by that name. More recently, the inquiry continues in tracts such as Laura Underkuffler's *The Idea of Property: Its Meaning and Power*.

What is liberty? That issue focused Mills's attention in his 1859 masterpiece. Isaiah Berlin later reexamined the concept in his celebrated work, *Liberty*.

Or what is law? H. L. A. Hart's *The Concept of Law* was born out of that philosophical investigation. Subsequently, Ronald Dworkin explored the idea in *Law's Empire* and elsewhere.

Many other examples of writings on fundamental concepts abound.

Yet, for all that has been said about dissent – in books, articles, judicial opinions, and in the popular culture – it is remarkable that no one has devoted much, if any, attention to explaining what dissent is or what we intend to convey when we invoke it. No one has attempted to sketch its philosophical, linguistic, legal, or cultural meanings or usages. Again, as a concept, dissent is taken for granted, as if we should all recognize it immediately when we see or hear it.

By that measure, a dictionary definition of "dissent" should confirm what we purportedly know. Deriving from the Latin verb dissentire ("to differ in sentiment"), the term is defined as "opposition to a proposal or resolution" or "a difference of opinion," or "a disagreement." In light of the many contexts in which the word "dissent" may be used, the *Oxford English Dictionary* definition is overinclusive. For example, in familial disputes – a daughter says to her mother, "You're wrong" – there is surely disagreement, but is there necessarily dissent? Or if after watching a performance of Luciano Pavarotti, an opera lover asserted that Pavarotti was the best singer in the world and his friend were to voice a different opinion – "Jose Carreras made a much better Rudolfo" – would we refer to this difference as an instance of dissent? On the one hand, if we examined the matter analytically, the answer to these questions might possibly be "yes." On the other hand, if we thought of the matter linguistically, the answer would probably be "no."

Additionally, the *OED* definition suffers from underinclusiveness. "Opposition to a proposal or resolution" does not seem either extensive enough or strong enough to encompass various concepts that we might well understand as aspects of dissent, such as "provocation," "defiance," "civil disobedience," "destruction," or "rebellion." Moreover, unless the phrase "proposal or resolution" is read quite broadly, in which case its linguistic purchase is diminished, the definition could not begin to capture more generalized instances of opposition to a societal way of life or a cultural attitude or aesthetic.

The gospel of the dictionary notwithstanding, we might wonder whether we have a real understanding of what dissent is or how we use it. We might wonder if we have an informed sense of what it means or how we speak of it in our modern culture of political pluralism, societal toleration, and corporate exploitation. And, should we pause to think seriously about dissent, we might also wonder whether we have a fully informed idea of how it relates to, and operates in, our system of freedom of expression, be it political, religious, or other.

This philosophical, linguistic, cultural, and jurisprudential problem becomes acute when we ask a simple question: Who qualifies as a dissenter? Some candidates are said to be obvious: Socrates, Jesus, Joan of Arc, Luther, Thoreau, Gandhi, Martin Luther King, Margaret Sanger, or Christopher Hitchins. Other candidates seem far less apparent: John Wilkes Booth, Lee Harvey Oswald, Huey P. Newton, Patty Hearst, "The Unabomber," and the Columbine High School killers. Similarly, what about Zacarias Moussaoui, the 9/11 terrorist, or Jared Loughner, the man charged with the attempted assassination of Congresswoman Gabrielle Giffords? Can we label all of these people dissenters? If so, why? If not, why not? The dictionary definition does little to help us resolve such questions.

If some of those names seem anomalous as dissenters, this points to a related question: What qualifies as dissenting activity? To be clear, the issue is *not* the legality of an activity, but whether it may reasonably be labeled an act of dissent. When violence is added to the conceptual mix, the question becomes more complicated. Just consider a sampling of views from some of our learned contributors to this book:

> *Frederick Schauer:* "You can be a violent dissenter as well as a non-violent dissenter."

> *Michael Walzer:* "Violent action, I suppose, could be an expression of dissent, but it goes beyond dissent. Dissent is a form of political, intellectual engagement, and violence is something different. It can be motivated by dissent. [John Wilkes Booth's crime was] an act of murder. I'm not sure how to draw the line."

> *Steven K. Green:* "I think Booth was expressing a form of dissent."

> *Ralph Nader:* "Violence cannot be called dissent. It has to be called violence."

> *Martha C. Nussbaum:* "If we took the anarchist who assassinated Garfield, I think that was a case of dissent, since he was clearly motivated by political opinions. And the assassination of Julius Caesar, that's an absolutely crystal clear case of dissent."

> *Nadine Strossen:* "Violent confrontation? I think that goes beyond the pale" of dissent.

Again, asking if violent words and deeds can be categorized as dissent is quite different from asking whether those words or deeds should be protected under law. The first inquiry is a conceptual one, whereas the second is a legal one.

Importantly, the meanings and usages of dissent cannot be derived entirely from what the law permits. If dissent is explained in something other than very narrow ways, it is possible for a culture to value it and yet proscribe it, at least at the outset. For example, only consider the civil rights demonstrations of the 1960s. Many of them began as breaches of state criminal and civil codes, but were later legitimated under the First Amendment. By comparison, other acts of civil disobedience, although clearly viewed as dissent, were not legitimated under our supreme law.

Moving from the criminal to the cultural, yet other questions surface. For example, can a commercial for-profit corporation ever be a dissenter? Does the profit motive change the analytical equation? If so, why? If not, why not? Here, too, the contrasting views of contemporary noted figures and respected scholars are instructive:

Michael Walzer: "I doubt it, but I don't know. Given the character of corporate behavior in a capitalist society, it is a legitimate suspicion that it is only acting to profit-maximize. But that's only a suspicion. It might not be true."

Kent Greenawalt: "In theory it could happen, yes, but it seems very unlikely in our culture. Could their politically oriented speech be deemed dissent? Yes, if the company really took on a dominant policy."

Sue Curry Jansen: "I'm really ambiguous here. I want to say 'yes' on some levels, but on other levels . . . one has to probe very deeply into what's behind" corporate dissent.

Of course, still other nagging questions remain. Such matters are the focus of what follows in this book.

At this juncture, a skeptical pragmatist may well ask: "So what?" What is the significance of a *conceptual* exploration of dissent? Unless notions of dissent and categories of legally protected acts are coextensive, why should we engage in "word games" or otherwise care about the meanings or usages of the word "dissent"?

This challenge must be taken seriously and answered. As a preliminary matter, our undertaking promotes several different interests:

Intellectual Interests: Probing the concept of dissent may be a worthy enterprise in and of itself. For, as the adage goes, knowledge can be valued for knowledge's sake. Beyond the Platonic, however, there is the pragmatic. After all, how we conceptualize something influences how we react to or engage with it. That is, how we understand or use the term "dissent" will likely determine whether we value or devalue acts taken in its name. Our minds do not operate in a vacuum. To be clear about an idea is to be clear about its ramifications, philosophical and practical.

Linguistic Interests: Clarity in communication depends on some commonality of understanding. Effectual communication breaks down when the meanings and usages of words run rampant. Should propositions about dissent become unclear, several results could follow. If the notion of "dissent" were unduly limited, certain activities otherwise corresponding to it might be heedlessly devalued. Or if the term were used in too open-ended a fashion, the word might lose much conceptual or practical purchase. Or if "dissent" is irresponsibly ambiguous, that might prejudice how laws are applied to dissenting activities.

Societal Interests: There is sociological significance in deciphering whether and when the idea of dissent shapes community norms. Some notions of dissent – from property destruction in the name of anarchy, to cross burning in the name of bigotry, to corporate appropriation in the name of profiteering – might fit awkwardly, if at all, with the cultural values commonly associated with dissent.

Legal Interests: Answers to the question "What is dissent?" may have implications for legal determinations running the gamut from criminality to constitutionality. Whether there is an exculpatory defense to criminal charges or civil liabilities, whether there is a reduction of a criminal penalty or a civil fine, or whether an otherwise prohibited activity becomes constitutionally protected may well hinge on the understanding and appreciation of dissent by a police officer, prosecutor, judge, jury, governor, or even the president. In a sense, branding something as dissent increases the chances that it might be legitimated.

Hence, the need to be more clear-minded about this phenomenon we call dissent cannot be gainsaid. For not every disagreement or disbelief, purposeful protest or unintentional transgression, symbolic or aesthetic expression, corporate or commercial contestation, criminal wrong or politically violent conduct, or religious action taken in God's name ought to be tagged dissent. We trust most would agree. And yet, there can be no significant agreement if there is not some real measure of meaning or regularity of usage.

It is just that conceptual yardstick that this work proffers. In that sense, *On Dissent* is a book like no other. It brings into bold relief what has heretofore been unseen.

CHAPTER I

FROM JUDICIAL DISSENT TO PEACEFUL PROTEST

"Holmes, J., dissenting." That phrase is known by every student of the law. Among other things, it refers to a 1919 opinion that Justice Oliver Wendell Holmes penned in a famous First Amendment case – *Abrams v. United States*. The "best test of truth," the jurist opined therein, "is the power of thought to get itself accepted in the competition of the market." This celebrated paean to free speech liberty arose in the context of a dissent Holmes wrote on behalf of several Russian dissidents charged with violating the Sedition Act of 1918. He strongly opposed the Court's affirmation of a twenty-year sentence for the dissidents, who had distributed leaflets calling for a general strike to prevent shipment of arms to Russia. In this and other matters, Holmes "wholly disagree[d] with the argument of the government" and the majority of the Justices.

Notably, judicial dissent is a case of institutionalized opposition. That is, dissent is a vital part of the tradition of appellate decision making. In that sense, it may not operate in the same conceptual quarters as other far riskier acts that might be labeled as dissent. Still, whatever one makes of this phenomenon, few would contest that it is a paradigmatic example of dissent, if only because it is expressly labeled so. However the word "dissent" is used, then, it must at least include an expression of judicial divergence from the majority opinion of a court.

But what if we push the conceptual envelope somewhat beyond the obvious? How far can we go and retain an unquestionable nexus to a judicial dissent? Let us look at two more examples.

In 1962, sixty or so members of the Students for a Democratic Society (SDS) met at a labor camp outside of Port Huron, Michigan, to finalize a provocative "agenda for a generation." Active in civil rights, campus reform, and peace movements, these students debated a fifty-page, single-spaced draft of a manifesto that would come to be known as *The Port Huron Statement*. This document addressed the major issues facing the youth of their time – everything from the Vietnam War and the atom bomb to racial justice and poverty, the tyranny of technology, and apathy and administrative paternalism on college campuses. "We are the People of this Generation," they wrote, "looking uncomfortably to the world we inherit." They offered their "appeal" as "an effort in understanding and changing the conditions of humanity in the late twentieth century, an effort rooted in the ancient, still unfulfilled conception of man attaining determining influence over his circumstances of life." Calling on America to adopt a number of domestic and international reforms, the Statement concluded: "If we appear to seek the unattainable . . . then let it be known that we do so to avoid the unimaginable." So far as the notion of dissent is concerned, does this idealized student activist manifesto fall within the same or similar conceptual parameters as institutionalized judicial dissent?

Moving to more contemporary times, consider the following. In 2011, a woman stood in a crowd assembled in front of the White House. Along with other members of the Tea Party, she opposed the evils of big government. She held up a placard depicting Uncle Sam, his finger extended as if to command the sign's directive: "Stop Shredding Our Constitution." A passerby might characterize the woman as engaging in a case of peaceful protest. Have we here another clear example of dissent?

To begin to answer these questions, it is necessary to do some preliminary analytical and linguistic spadework. That is, how do we *conceptualize* the issues raised by such questions and how do we *speak* of them?

Returning to our judicial example, we ask what attributes are essential to it that permit us to postulate that it is a paradigm of dissent. This claim derives from three key characteristics: that the expression is *intentional*; that it is *critical*; and that it is *public*. In abbreviated form, these attributes can be understood as follows:

1. *Intention:* a knowing determination or resolve to think, believe, speak, or act in a certain way, with a reasonable awareness and understanding of the probable significance, import, or consequences of that expression or action; a subjective understanding that one is purposefully communicating.

2. *Criticism:* an unfavorable evaluation, adverse judgment, or disapproving opinion of a law, policy, practice, or position established by an authority structure, whether legal, religious, scientific, social, or cultural.
3. *Public:* not confined to the private realm, but instead meaningfully exposed to an authority structure, to members of a group or community, or in a venue open to others.

By these measures, the Port Huron and Tea Party examples constitute dissent analogous to the judicial example. The SDS members unquestionably intended to openly disseminate their highly critical views of the then-prevailing laws and norms of the American "establishment." Similarly, the Tea Party protestor acted purposefully in a public forum to communicate her disapproval of the national government's disregard of her constitutional rights, as she understood them. Hence, the conceptual fit works analytically. The fit with language usage, however, is not as apparent.

When we think of the Port Huron and Tea Party examples and how we speak of them, the word most likely to be used to describe them is "protest." That is, assume someone were to ask, "What is the *Port Huron Statement*?" or "What is the SDS doing?" The answer would, in one way or another, probably refer to protest. So, too, with our earlier allusion to the passerby who inquired about what the Tea Party woman was doing in front of the White House. The expected reply would be: "She's protesting." By contrast, we would not speak of the judicial example in the same way. We would not call it an act of protest; or if we did, we would do so awkwardly. How strange it would be to state: "Holmes, J., protesting." Why is this so? One primary reason is that judicial dissent is an institutionalized form of disagreement, in the sense that it is expected, accepted, and normalized.

These clues from ordinary language prompt us to examine the relationship between dissent and protest. Are they synonymous? Are they similar? Are there important differences between them? Without venturing into an extended exegesis on the meanings and usages of "protest," it is evident that there is a deep connection between the two terms, at least under certain conditions.

While it would be odd to refer to judicial dissents as protests, it would be equally odd to cabin the concept of dissent to the judicial realm. For example, if someone were to ask, "What has happened to dissent in America?," would anyone reasonably assume that the query was directed to the business of appellate judges? Or if someone were to declare, "Proposed antiterrorism legislation will criminalize dissent," would we imagine that the declarant was not addressing public protest? In the same regard, consider what we would make of a book with the following title: *Dissent in America: The Voices That Shaped a Nation – 400 Years of Speeches, Sermons, Arguments, Articles, Letters, and Songs That Made a Difference*. The audience for this book would immediately understand the connection implied between dissent and protest.

We can now breathe more easily that the Port Huron and Tea Party examples of protest can fall readily under both the logical and linguistic umbrella of dissent. That said, there is something regarding the word "dissent" that has a more dignified appreciation about it. While "dissent" and "protest" may be seen as conceptual cousins, the former strikes us as the nobler cousin. The reader need only recall our Prologue's discussion of the elevated values equated with "dissent." Although the same ideals might arguably be logically aligned with "protest," they are much less likely to be associated linguistically with it. In that sense, "dissent" may generally be perceived as indicating "protest-plus" – that is, a "plus" that suggests societal toleration. As we will see in later chapters, the more the notion of dissent moves away from normative acceptance, the more we are likely to devalue the term and even forsake it.

୦୫ ଧୀ

Our abbreviated presentation of the three key attributes of dissent was adequate for our general inquiry into the subject. Now, however, we need to take a more particularized and nuanced look at those attributes. To get a better sense of things, let us tease out the subtler aspects of our investigation.

INTENTION

It would be peculiar to think that someone could dissent without some meaningful intent to do so. Can there be unknowing dissent or accidental dissent? In other words, must dissent be rooted in the mind? To help us along, let us call on some expert witnesses.

For many, intention is a categorical imperative for dissent:

Hans Linde: "To be dissent, an action must have communicative intent, or it's just something that is a non-conforming act."

Jon O. Newman: "Intention is key to dissent. If an act or expression is accidental or inadvertent, it doesn't register on the scale of dissent at all."

Martha Nussbaum: "I think intention is an essential characteristic. . . . Dissent involves a willingness to take responsibility for what you say and do, and therefore it does require that you know what you're doing or that you have some view of what you're doing. There is no unaware dissenter."

To others, intention is also a key attribute of dissent, even though that intent may not be as apparent or robust as one might think. Take, for example, the following point:

Howard Zinn: "I believe a dissenter has a reasonable awareness and understanding of the significance and consequences of his actions. . . . There are different degrees of consciousness about the importance of your dissenting action. There are experienced dissenters who know, understand, and have thought about it. And there are people who act without thinking too much about it. . . . But dissent would have to have some element of social consciousness, even if it were very limited."

The clear consensus, therefore, is that intention is vital to any meaningful notion of dissent. But to probe this point even further, consider a few examples. Imagine a group of people brandishing pro-union signs in front of an anti-union shop in a town largely hostile to the union cause. Among other things, the signs read: "Don't support this union buster!" and "Help close this anti-union shop down!" Passersby would assume that those carrying the placards are union sympathizers and, therefore, dissenters. But what if the sign-carriers were homeless people hired by the union? What if it were entirely irrelevant to these hired hands what the signs said? What if, so long as they were paid, they would be happy to carry anti-union signs? In the eyes of the passersby, the actual intent of the "protesters" is of no moment because their audience has no knowledge of it. But let us not stop there. What if a television reporter were to interview our "protesters," and in the process learn of their true intent? When that report is later aired on television or YouTube, the viewers would see the same acts through entirely different lenses and might well refuse to label such actions as dissent.

Consider another telling example offered by Justice William Brennan in *Texas v. Johnson*, the 1989 flag dese- cration case. The jurist hypothesized a situation in which a tired person might drag a flag in the mud, but with no inten- tion of making any kind of political statement. Would this lackadaisical action amount to dissent? Would it be enough if such unintentional desecration was perceived as a form of dissent by onlookers or even only by government reg- ulators? Put differently, what is the conceptual touchstone for dissent – the intent of the speaker, the perception of the audience, or the regulatory purpose of the government? For if the understanding of either the audience or government controls, then one might conclude that unintentional dissent is, indeed, possible.

In this regard, one authority, while conceding the impor- tance of a dissenter's intentionality, contests its categorical status:

> *Steven Shiffrin*: "I do not believe that intention is a neces- sary condition for dissent, because somebody can engage in an action that is perceived as criticizing existing customs, habits,

institutions, traditions, or authorities, even though that is not intended.... To the extent that [dragging the flag in the mud] is penalized because of the message that is communicated, it is an attempt to stifle dissent, even though a criticism was not intended.... I do think that there are greater qualities of dissent when it is intended to be dissent. But there are circumstances in which there is no intent, but there is regulation of the communication, and I believe that can be a regulation of dissent."

Among other things, what is intriguing about Shiffrin's view is that, when he characterizes the flag-dragging hypothetical as a regulation of dissent, he puts far less importance on the flag-bearer's intention to dissent or the onlookers' perception of dissent than on the government's purpose to stifle dissent. Hence, the presence of dissent is not primarily to be determined by either the intent of the speaker or that of the audience, but rather by the intent of the government (insofar as that intent is inferred from the government's regulatory purposes or practices). Ostensibly, Shiffrin's shift away from a focus on speaker intent to a focus on government intent presumably aims to prevent any "chilling effects" of flag desecration laws on the future actions of dissenters who knowingly use the flag as a symbol in their political protests. Even so, what is notable in Shiffrin's position is that *intention* remains a key attribute for dissent; *whose* intention is the debatable point.*

---

* Couched another way, Professor Shiffrin's captivating commentary has less to do with a purported dissenter and his expressive actions than with the government and its purported unlawful actions. Thus, if one were to apply the same logic to Justice Brennan's flag hypothetical, we assume that Professor Shiffrin would likewise argue that it is of no moment that the flag-bearer's conduct might not be defined as speech within the

Distancing our understanding of dissent from a dissenter's intentionality can prove problematic, however, and for several sound reasons. First, without an intentional decision to break away from the status quo enough to object to it in some meaningful fashion, a dissenter becomes indistinguishable from someone who is merely uncomfortable with the existing ethos and weakly expresses some dissatisfaction with it.

Second, assume that an individual is intuitively repelled by some establishment policy or practice, but cannot immediately explain fleshed-out reasons for that reaction. Nonetheless, as Professor Zinn suggested, eventually there would need to be some more developed intention before he or she acted in a way that would be understood as dissent. As the example of the pro-union "protesters" reveals, what we later learn about the real purposes behind any action determines how we characterize it.

Third, it is possible, as in the flag desecration illustration, that a person may unwillingly "criticize" an authority's position, and it might have communicative impact on an audience that understands the expression or action as dissent. But any public misimpression could be corrected – either directly, if questioned, by the person's persuasive denial of

meaning of the First Amendment. For Brennan, by contrast, it was of decisive moment, insofar as unintentional conduct would not rise to the level of speech. In sum, the problem with Shiffrin's argument is that it goes too far. It does this because its focus is less definitional than normative; it would trade virtually all definitional concerns for parameters on government power.

any intentional dissent, or indirectly by the person's compliance with the law.

Fourth, without the intent to communicate a message and an appreciation of how that message will be likely be understood, it is not clear that an action can be billed as expressive conduct at all; in other words, the actor intends to convey no message. In this light, it seems curious to call an individual a dissenter if he or she acts without any intent to express a view that challenges or contests conventional positions.

Fifth, the way we use our language confirms much of this. For example, if we knew that the sign-carriers were entirely indifferent to the union cause, it would be odd to claim that they were pro-union dissenters. And if we knew that our flag-dragger did not intend to desecrate the flag, it would be strange to say: "Though he didn't realize it, Joe dissented when he accidentally dragged the flag in the mud." Or if someone were to say, "It was a case of accidental dissent," the chances are high that such a remark would be understood as flip or comical. Or to belabor the point, consider the oddity of asserting: "Justice Holmes dissented without intending to do so."

Finally, it is well to remember that analyzing such issues is not necessarily synonymous with how we might think of them in a court of law, among other places. Undoubtedly, there will be a category of instances where individual intention differs from public perception, as when passersby attribute dissenting status to the pro-union sign-carriers and the flag-desecrator. Here, perception would be buttressed by the way we commonly refer to such actions. Functionally speaking, the acts would fairly be classified as dissent, unless evidence of a contrary intent emerged to trump the original perception. In short, there may be circumstances in which true intent would yield to its functional equivalent. Either way, intention matters.

Important as we think intention is to any concept of dissent, it must work in tandem with the two other attributes we have identified, namely criticism that is made public. We now turn to the next attribute.

CRITICISM

Recall that the *Oxford English Dictionary* definition of dissent considers the term to be synonymous with "opposition," "disagreement," or "a difference of opinion." Such an adverse perspective, while in need of elaboration, is obvious to the meaning of dissent. For, to remove adversity from the concept of dissent would be to defang it. There must be something confrontational in a dissenting expression or act, even if the character and degree of that something remain to be discussed. Where there is pure consensus, there is no room for dissent; where there is approving compliance with orthodoxy or conventionality, there is no dissent.

It should not be surprising, then, to find a strong consensus among those who have thought through the issue that criticism is a sine qua non of dissent, as exemplified by the following commentaries:

Catharine MacKinnon: "The essence of dissent is about standing up to, confronting power. Dissent carries with it a critical stance toward existing structures of domination."

Steven Green: "Criticism is the heart of what dissent is all about. You can't be in agreement with something you disagree with. There can be degrees of agreement. But there needs to be a critique of what you find offensive or wrong as essential to dissent."

Ralph Nader: "Dissent involves expressions that challenge the status quo, entrenched power, the conventional wisdom. . . . Usually it's a challenge or opposition to a prevailing view or a prevailing power structure."

Michael Walzer: "I think dissent and criticism are virtually synonymous. If you are challenging, questioning . . . some conventional opinion, some standard doctrine of your society, you are also, in effect, criticizing it."

Given that criticism lies at the core of dissent, why is that so? Among other reasons, the attribute of criticism is vital because it serves to distinguish dissent from two other intellectual states of disagreement – doubt and disbelief. Surely, there is a relationship among doubt, disbelief, and dissent, but they ought not be viewed as simply interchangeable. Rather, they appear to fall on a conceptual and linguistic continuum, with doubt and disbelief quite often being antecedent stages to dissent.

One who doubts or disbelieves a proposition may merely question it or refuse to place stock in it; he or she need not expend more energy, engagement, or commitment on the point, and may suffer little, if any, risk of retribution. By contrast, one who dissents has arrived at a more significant critical engagement or conflict with the prevailing ethos, and may suffer real risk of retribution. Dissent adds fuel to the fire; it tends to be more active, vibrant, and confrontational than its two counterparts.

It was one thing for Martin Luther to doubt or disbelieve that the pope was the Vicar of Christ, but it was quite another thing for him to openly criticize in writing the pope's author- ity and the Church's abuses. Moreover, Luther's refusal to retract his *95 Theses* (1517) at the demand of Pope Leo X further exemplified his critical posture. His stance against religious and secular authorities resulted in his excommu- nication and his condemnation by Emperor Charles V as an outlaw. When Luther, the monk, moved from personal doubt and disbelief to public criticism, he became Luther, the Reformer. In the process, he traveled the road from doubt to dissent.

For our present purposes, what is crucial about Martin Luther's action is not only that it diverged from the pre- vailing religious norms, but also that he intended to criticize those norms openly. Mere divergence ought not be sufficient for dissent. Consider the following examples that address this point:

- A man walks down Hollywood Boulevard wearing an exceptionally gaudy green tie that features a scantily clad hula dancer. He intends to make no political or aesthetic statement; he simply prefers bizarre ties, in much the same way that he likes to put hot sauce on pancakes when breakfasting in a restaurant. Assuredly, the tie diverges from even the Hollywood norm of style; but because he intends no public criticism of conventional fashion norms, we would not bill his choice in clothing an act of dissent. Ironically, his eccentric lifestyle benefits from the social toleration fostered by a culture of dissent, which suits him just fine.

- Assume the year is 1975, and John Doe is in the Navy where he has served with distinction for fifteen years. In order to secure a promotion and pay upgrade, he must obtain a security clearance, for which he first must answer a series of questions. In the course of the interview, he is asked if he is homosexual, and he responds honestly in the affirmative. (If it had been decades later, he would have willingly abided by the "Don't Ask, Don't Tell" policy and kept his sexual orientation a secret.) John has no desire to buck the system or to make a public political statement; neither is he concerned whether other homosexuals are able to obtain security clearances; he simply wants to comply in the hope that he might be promoted. As a result of his integrity, John is summarily dismissed, but is nonetheless honorably discharged. Obviously, he is quite distressed by this, but takes the bitter pill rather than making a spectacle of himself. Here, John's sexuality diverged from the norm, and he communicated that to his superiors. While he came close to the door of dissent, he did not cross the threshold because he lacked any specific intention to be critical of the status quo.

- Until June 1967, the "mixing of the races" in interracial or interethnic couplings and marriages was considered to be socially abhorrent and was legally prohibited in many American states. Before that date, such couples made more than a political statement – they put their very lives in jeopardy. In *Loving v. Virginia* (1967), the U.S. Supreme Court held that the state's antimiscegenation law was unconstitutional. With the passage of time after

the decision, general attitudes toward such mixed marriages eased, by and large. Assume, then, that a contemporary Black Power group openly rails against the "evils
of miscegenation," arguing that mixed-race relationships
dilute the purity and splendor of the black race. Such a
view would be seen in many places as offensive to prevailing racial attitudes; indeed, harkening back to *Loving*,
some might view such admonitions as racist. Nonetheless, there can be no serious question that the group's
criticism amounts to dissent. Among other matters, the
point here is that the concept of dissent has no ideological
favorites. To drive that point home even further, imagine
that a "free love" group protests against the prosecution of a forty-year-old woman who had non-forcible sex
with a twelve-year-old boy. At a press conference, the
group openly lauds pedophilia and calls for its decrimi-
nalization. Far from devaluing the protest's status as dissent, the highly offensive character of the expression only
enhances its credentials.

All of these examples, in one way or another, pit individuals with divergent views against dominant forms of majoritarian will. And it is true that typically the criticism that feeds
dissent targets majoritarian norms or power structures. But
this need not always be the case. For context very much
defines the character of the activity in question. Just as we
commonly witness dissent playing out along a minority-
majority axis, so it may play out in a similar way entirely
within a minority community. That is, there may be dis-
sention within the ranks of a minority group itself. What is
interesting is that the opposition of an individual within such
a group might actually align with the prevailing orthodoxy

of the dominant majority that alienates that group. In other words, in the minority community he or she is a dissenter, while in the majority community he or she is a conformist as to that particular issue.

Reconsider the former example of the Black Power organization that abhors mixed-race couplings and marriages. Assume that a member of that group holds firmly to all of its other tenets, but believes that its pure-race creed is bigoted. At a series of meetings, the individual berates his colleagues for their misguided opinions and insists on the rectification of their insupportable public stance. Such fervent criticism of the Black Power organization's ideology is clearly dissent within that community, notwithstanding the minority status of the group within the national polity. It might be said that this scenario does nothing other than transport the minority-majority axis from a macro-context into a micro-context. There is great merit in this observation, and it highlights the significant, albeit contextualized, role of criticism as an attribute of dissent.

Only recall the strong consensus that we earlier identified as to to the essential connection between criticism and dissent. That there should be such a consensus ought not be surprising. After all, there is nothing particularly controversial about the idea of criticism in the abstract. Indeed, up to this point, the concept of criticism seems a rather tame one, suggesting little more, if anything, than an adverse mental act or verbal expression. Such a tame concept of criticism might, nevertheless, be synonymous with dissent. For example, think of a religiously inspired protestor in front of the New York statehouse who condemns same-sex marriage as sinful and perverse. Or imagine a citizen at a New England town hall meeting who stands up to deliver a diverging opinion on municipal zoning policies. Or consider a citizen group that petitions the Congress for a redress of environmental grievances. Although such practices could produce harsh punitive results in totalitarian countries and cultures, in modern democratic societies such criticism typically is socially tolerated and legally protected.

Even in the contemporary United States, however, criticism has its limits. There is no blank check to be critical in all places at all times and in all manners. Criticism that is mental, verbal, peaceful, and performed in certain settings is easy to defend as a vital criterion of dissent. But what if that criticism manifests itself in more robust ways, in ways that move beyond words to action, beyond peaceful protest to civil unrest? Would that criticism also be billed as dissent? And would that dissent also be socially tolerated and legally protected? These are questions that deserve consideration, and such examination will be given in due course. At this juncture, it suffices merely to flag the issue that the meaning and value of dissent are connected to and influenced by its manifestations. Nonetheless, it cannot be gainsaid that the attribute of criticism lies at the core of any expression or action worthy of the name of dissent.

PUBLIC

Beyond intention and criticism, what does the public character of expression add to the mix, such that we might deem it an essential attribute of dissent? After all, when we think of historically significant expressions of dissent in America, we would come quickly to Martin Luther King's "I Have a Dream" speech, delivered against the backdrop of the Lincoln Memorial. That August 23, 1963 address and many others by Dr. King are canonical instances of dissent. His declarations were quintessential illustrations of publicly speaking truth to power. In that regard, consider the following example of Martin Luther King's thought expressed in his own words:

> [There is,] particularly in the young generation, a spirit of dissent that raged from superficial disapproval of the old values to total commitment to wholesale, drastic and immediate social reform. Yet all of it was dissent. Their voice is still a minority; but united with millions of black protesting voices, it has become a sound of distant thunder increasing in volume with the gathering of storm clouds. This dissent is America's hope . . . America has not yet changed because so many think it need not change, but this is the illusion of the damned. America must change because twenty-three million black citizens will no longer live supinely in a wretched past. They have left the valley of despair; they have found strength in the struggle; and whether they live or die, they shall never crawl nor retreat again. Joined by white allies, they will shake the prison walls until they fall. America must change.

It would be most curious to ask if such a forceful call to action should be considered dissent. Nonetheless, there may be conceptual warrant to do so. Dr. King's statement was clearly intentional and obviously critical. But does it matter that his remarks, found among his personal papers, were published posthumously? In this regard, consider the following possibilities:

- What if King never planned to deliver or publish his statement? For example, what if the statement and the longer essay from which it was drawn were intended to be no more than an extended private diary entry?
- Or what if, in the days before the Presidential Records Act (1978) and the Freedom of Information Act (1966), King had sent his statement to then-President Lyndon B. Johnson with the admonition that it be shared with no one else?
- Alternatively, what if King had planned to make it public during his lifetime, but only anonymously?

To align these considerations with our earlier example of judicial dissent, what about Justice Louis Brandeis's dissent in the 1926 case of *Ruthenberg v. Michigan*, an opinion that was, for jurisdictional reasons, published for the first time nearly seven decades after the jurist's death?

These and other inquiries prompt us to analyze in a nuanced manner the connection between the character of dissent and its public footprint. How essential is it that critical remarks made intentionally be also conveyed in some public fashion? Many who have seriously considered the issue hold that public status is a core attribute of dissent. Among them are the following:

Todd Gitlin: "Public is clearly fundamental."

Hans Linde: "We can begin by referring only to an expressed or visible disagreement and not a silent disagreement."

Jon O. Newman: "The public character is essential. Otherwise, like the proverbial tree that falls in the forest, dissent won't make a noise."

Sut Jhally: "Dissent, without it being public, is something else.... The public nature of it – and being able to stand behind it and to think about it as an intentional act – are key aspects of dissent. Otherwise, it's a private, conscious objection, and you can wrestle with those things in your mind, but to the extent that dissent is worth thinking about in philosophical or legal terms, it has to make its way into the public realm."

Dissent is correlated with public manifestation of some sort for several reasons. First, without a certain degree of public recognition, intentional criticism is likely to be completely ineffective. Solitary dissent is more akin to a cerebral act than to a political or social one. To have any political or social valence, dissent requires some public exposure; otherwise, there is no real potential to convey opposition to power structures or to facilitate social or cultural change.

Second, dissent, at least in its more vibrant forms, entails some degree of risk of adverse consequences. That risk might run the gamut from public condemnation and social ostracism to personal injury and imprisonment. Speaking truth to power, after all, can have its price. But such dissent is valued precisely because one steps up and assumes the risk. If expression or action is entirely immune from any public scrutiny, there is little, if any, risk incurred. Speaking privately to friends or to ideological cohorts, then, lacks both the edge and the peril of dissent.

Third, implicit in the idea of speaking truth to power is the notion of personal integrity – that is, assuming ownership of one's views. Whether it be Sophocles' Antigone challenging King Creon's edict or Muhammad Ali refusing military induction during the Vietnam War, the public character of dissent can buttress the righteousness of claims. Only consider Norman Rockwell's 1943 painting, *Freedom of Speech*, which illustrates a courageous figure standing up among his fellow citizens to express his opinions; this iconic image is so powerful because the man takes public ownership of his ideas, and thereby affirms the strength of his convictions.

The last point notwithstanding, there are instances in which we might find dissent even if one declines to "own" it, as in the case of anonymous dissent. As long as the criticism itself is public, there will be times when the identity of the critic need not be revealed. The history of early dissent in America, as described by Justice Hugo Black in *Talley v. California* (1960), illustrates the point. "Anonymous pamphlets, leaflets, brochures, and even books have played an important role in the progress of mankind. Persecuted groups and sects from time to time throughout history have been able to [anonymously] criticize oppressive practices and laws," Black wrote for the majority. "The obnoxious press licensing law of England, which was also enforced on the colonies," he added, "was due in part to the knowledge that exposure of the names of printers, writers and distributors would lessen the circulation of literature critical of the government. . . . Even the *Federalist Papers*, written in favor of the adoption of our Constitution, were published under fictitious names." Thus, Black concluded, "[i]t is plain that anonymity has been assumed for the most constructive purposes." Because of this tradition, anonymous oppositional expression continues to be constitutionally protected, even in non-repressive times.

While we see anonymity as an understandable, albeit limited, qualification of the public character of dissent, should we so qualify criticism that is not intended to be shared with others, or that is shared with a single or a small number of private recipients? In the first instance, recall our example of Dr. King's private diary entries. For Professor Nadine Strossen, the secret character of diary writing disqualifies it as dissent: "Writing in your own diary would not count for me. Talking to yourself would not count for me." This is an entirely plausible position, because all of the foregoing explanations rationalizing the public character of dissent are undermined.

That said, if one pauses for a moment to reflect on the possible purposes for diary entries, the matter becomes more complicated. Although a diary may be no more than a record of personal history and may forever remain private, sometimes a diary accidentally becomes public or is intended to become public after death – the author "speaks from the grave," as it were. In the latter cases, what was heretofore private becomes public. When this occurs, "that might get much closer to, if not arrive into, the area of dissent," Judge Jon Newman reasons. "Almost everyone understands that once you write something down, there's a risk it will become public. . . . So, unless you go to extraordinary lengths to safeguard the secrecy of your criticism, there is a risk." Such a risk, of course, was entirely foreseeable to Dr. King, who had every reason to believe that his private papers, especially searing criticism of the established order, would be published after his death. By contrast, the same would not necessarily hold true for nonpublic figures who could not reasonably expect that their private musings would have public value. In short, although perhaps we can imagine diary entries by public figures being characterized as dissent, it is far more difficult to do so for private figures who engage in such practices.

In the second instance, remember Dr. King's hypothetical letter to President Johnson. Here the fly in the conceptual ointment is the meaning of "public" – that is, how public must criticism be to count as dissent? Can exposure to a single person or to a small group of persons be sufficient for the public character of dissent? If by "public" we understand criticism that is open to general observation, then King's letter to Johnson would not constitute dissent. Analytically and linguistically, it is difficult to stretch this meaning of "public" to fit private criticism intended to remain so. The same would likely hold for a critical communication conveyed to a small group.

Even so, for the Johnson letter hypothetical, we might see the need for a narrow exception to the public character of dissent. In that scenario, Dr. King purposefully directs his criticism to a politically powerful authority figure, and thereby exposes his expression to possible public awareness and subjects himself to a potential risk of retribution. The case should be no different if King's private letter were addressed to a small number of Johnson's cabinet, since this group would be perceived as one that King intends to criticize. (Indeed, such "dissent," if it can rightfully be called that, is the mainstay of diplomatic envoys.) Of course, the same cannot be said if King's letter were sent, instead, to a sympathetic fellow clergyman.

Because our conceptual enterprise is often context-dependent, it should be noted that there are other situations in which expression would likely be deemed dissent, even if it is not otherwise public. This is most likely to be the case where opposition occurs in a totalitarian or otherwise highly repressive regime that is, where an open act of dissent could well be tantamount to suicide. Just consider the practical impossibility of public dissent in the contexts of Athens in the fifth and fourth centuries BC, or in Muslim countries in the early Middle Ages, or in fifteenth-century Spain, or in seventeenth-century Holland or England, or in eighteenth-century France, or in twentieth-century Stalinist Russia or Nazi Germany, or in modern-day Iran. In any of these or other such contexts, an underground oppositional culture, so fraught with danger that it is not publicized, might nonetheless be labeled a dissenting one. By stark contrast, where a society is free and democratic, such private acts stand to lose their currency as dissent.

There is a related possibility, one especially known to philosophers, literary figures, and religious writers alike. In repressive periods, the need to express critical opinion might most safely be done by writing esoterically – that is, between the lines. On the one hand, Leo Strauss tells us, "it is a safe venture to tell the truth one knows to benevolent and trust-worthy acquaintances." On the other hand, the possibility of persecution will prompt "a man of independent thought

[to] utter his views in public . . . provided he moves with cir-
cumspection. He can utter them in print without incurring
any danger, provided he is capable of writing between the
lines." Interestingly, with such esoteric expression, a message might be, at one and the same time, a public act and
private dissent.

∞ ∞

 The three attributes – intention, criticism, and public –
lie at the conceptual and linguistic core of dissent. If one or
more of these characteristics were not found in an expression or action, it would be improbable, if not impossible,
to name it dissent. Additionally, the more the expression or
action moves away from these characteristics in their most
pristine form, the less likely it is to be labeled dissent. Of
course, when these three attributes are combined with others, an activity could still qualify as dissent; indeed, in certain
instances, it will be an even stronger candidate for dissent.
It is to just such matters that we turn next.

CHAPTER II

FROM CIVIL TO UNCIVIL DISOBEDIENCE

The elevated spirit of dissent is captured not only by lawful protest, but sometimes also by its opposite. Only reflect on the revered admonitions and actions of Henry David Thoreau, Mohandas Gandhi, and Martin Luther King. Or consider the message of a noted AIDS activist, Aldyn McKean: "I have an arrest record for civil disobedience that spans 23 years and covers seven states, the District of Columbia, and one foreign country. However, I never go to a demonstration to get arrested; I go to bring about change, and am willing to risk arrest to produce that desired change."

Quintessentially, McKean is an activist – someone who takes unlawful action to advance his sense of social justice. But not all civil disobedience is cut from the same conceptual cloth. Take, for example, an instance of principled inaction, as when someone unlawfully declines to serve in the military. Nearly a half-century ago, on April 28, 1967, a famous American boxer publicly refused induction into the Army, this at the height of the Vietnam War. Citing religious beliefs, Muhammad Ali boldly reaffirmed what he had declared earlier: "I ain't got no quarrel with them Vietcong." This unlawful act of conscientious protest cost him dearly: he was stripped of his championship title and barred by every state athletic commission from fighting for almost four years. Moreover, he was indicted and convicted of violating the federal draft law. Absent a Supreme Court ruling reversing his conviction on technical grounds, the widely spurned Ali would have gone to prison for five years.

Dissent, however, is not always lofty and proper. Civil disobedience is not always *civil*. Sometimes, in the rough and tumble of protest, agitation and antagonism hang in the air. This has been apparent in everything from the nineteenth-century Bostonians who boisterously condemned the murder of newspaper editor and abolitionist Elijah P. Lovejoy, to the twentieth-century Wobblies who belligerently protested to advance the cause of unskilled labor, to the twenty-first-century Occupy Wall Street demonstrators who vociferously campaigned against corporate greed and the excesses of capitalism. Profane, vulgar, and abusive language and gestures are often the very staple of public dissent in modern America.

At this point, all of this proves too much, for it presumes an obvious connection between dissent and civil disobedience. Before that nexus can be realized, it is first necessary to clear a little analytical brush; that is, we must first clarify our understanding of civil disobedience. When we pause, even briefly, to think about the history, meaning, and usage of the notion of civil disobedience, we begin to appreciate that the conceptual path from dissent to civil disobedience is not as straightforward as we might have assumed. In some senses, it is a tortuous path, one that twists and turns in different directions.

Many hold that civil disobedience is tantamount to dissent. The analytical rub, however, is what they understand civil disobedience to be. But there are multiple ways to conceive of civil disobedience. For example, one might consider civil disobedience to be:

1. Disobedience to the law that stems from the Thoreauvian notion of moral resistance to civil government, which is justified by an appeal to conscience and constrained by it alone.
2. Disobedience to the law that is truly "civil," insofar as the protester exercises respectful restraint and shuns unruly behavior.
3. Disobedience to the law that goes beyond civility, strictly understood, but transgresses it in a nonviolent way.
4. Disobedience to the law that crosses the line into threatening, intimidating, and even violent behavior.

These four discrete notions reveal that cavalierly equating civil disobedience with dissent is a risky enterprise that, if left unexamined, proves more perplexing than enlightening. Mindful of that conceptual backdrop, let us continue our exploration.

The father of the modern idea of "civil disobedience" never used that phrase in his seminal 1849 essay. The essay was not, as commonly thought, entitled *Civil Disobedience*; that title was assigned when it was reprinted in an 1866 collection of Henry David Thoreau's works four years after his death. For Thoreau, his ideas were best captured in the title he selected: *On Resistance to Civil Government*. The overarching point of the essay was that insofar as the constituted democratic processes failed to govern in accord with the dictates of conscience, a citizen was morally justified in breaching the law. In that original sense, "civil disobedience" was an intentional transgression of the laws of civil society. In other words, it was morally permissible to act unlawfully, to resist the rules established by civil government.

Some embrace this Thoreauvian notion of civil disobedience when they reflect on the phenomenon of dissent. Consider, for example, the following commentaries:

> *Steven Green*: "Civil disobedience is obviously dissent. Someone is willing to say: 'There are sanctions out there that I realize I'm transgressing.' Civil disobedience clearly recognizes the parameters of the legal and societal structure, and it's a public criticism of that structure."

> *Phil Donahue*: "Among the dissenting communities, civil disobedience is the noblest form of dissent – to actually break the law and pay for it."

These views take as a given that the idea of civil disobedience is synonymous with dissent. There is a willful breach of the law intended to oppose the established order in the name of a higher purpose. Such a notion, standing alone and without qualification, does not quarter civil disobedience to either civil or nonviolent acts. Whereas the disobedient's own conscience might constrain his or her behavior, the concept of civil disobedience, broadly defined, would not.

Some might counter that Thoreauvian disobedience must remain "civil," and therefore entirely respectful and constrained. Their understanding is one that is squarely anchored in the *civility* of the disobedient acts. Here the touchstone is the propriety with which a dissident manifests conscientious objection. Thus, while a citizen may disrespect the law, he or she should do so in a respectful way. This notion of civil disobedience is more readily apparent in what Thoreau did than in what he wrote. Simply consider his 1846 act of protest against the Mexican War when he refused to pay a poll tax that would support a cause to expand the domain of slavery. Such an idea of principled and restrained unlawful action paved the way for the kind of civil disobedience later developed by Gandhi and practiced by Dr. King.

By emphasizing civility, this second way of conceptualizing civil disobedience aims to cabin the potential reach of Thoreau's original notion of moral resistance to civil government. For, if left entirely unchecked, such conscientious resistance might cross the line from civil to uncivil, peaceful to riotous, and nonviolent to violent, all in the name of a "higher law." Therefore, some would exclude from the category of dissent all uncivil protest – aggressive and hostile name-calling, yelling obscenities, fist-shaking or other crude physical gestures – even when it never leads to violent confrontations:

> *Geoffrey Stone*: "To the extent that uncivil protest is intended to express criticism of government policy, I would say it is dissent. More people would say it's not dissent. . . . They would say that's raucous and disruptive disobedience."

> *Martha Nussbaum*: "As for uncivil protest, I think a lot of people would view that as possibly threatening, involving fighting words, so I think there would be much more doubt about whether that counts as dissent. And I would have that doubt,

depending on the context. My own view makes a very strong distinction between the expression of incivility in a general form and uncivil remarks targeted at an individual in a way that's threatening to that individual.... [For example,] at a gay pride parade, if a protester claims, 'You gays are ruining the family,' I would call that dissent.... But if we have a protester outside an abortion clinic who yells at a doctor, 'You should die,' that's not dissent. That's a clear case on the other side of the line."

For the critics of incivility, then, the distinction between civil and uncivil disobedience is the difference between respectful, orderly, and unintimidating dissent and its insolent, unruly, and threatening counterpart, which cannot even be tagged as dissent. Of course, some have a more elastic notion of civility, as exemplified by the following commentary:

Todd Gitlin: "Clearly, civil disobedience constitutes dissent. The sit-in is a classic or prototypical example of effective dissent, because it was non-violent and therefore constituted an invitation to the adversary to think of [the dissident] as a potential ally and co-member of society. [It involves] the capacity to mobilize a symbolism that generates sympathy and triggers a general recognition of what was at stake in the act: 'These people believe in constitutional rights, and by God it's horrible and unjust that they've been deprived of them, and they're acting in a reasonable way to produce what they want, and therefore I support them.' That's the chain of invitations that a sit-in offers."

In contrast, not all who equate dissent with civil disobedience would yield the point simply because incivilities have entered the equation. They might recognize that improprieties could be dishonorable, or tactically and strategically unproductive; in their calculus, however, uncivil disobedience intended as criticism targeting the established order nonetheless remains dissent:

> *Geoffrey Stone*: "I would clearly regard as dissent . . . raucous demonstrations that were intended to disrupt. The key is that the behavior for which you are punished has to be intended to express criticism of the government."

> *Howard Zinn*: "A parade or demonstration accompanied by incivilities? I've been at a number of those, and yes, I would consider them dissenting activities. As a tactical matter, I am not happy with people who yell obscenities. But certainly I would consider all of that to fall within the definition of dissent."

> *Cornel West*: "There are different forms of dissent that are of a higher moral character than others. But I don't want to confine dissent solely to those forms that have higher moral character. So uncivil disobedience is still a form of dissent."

Notably, even those who would sacrifice civility on the altar of dissent are unlikely to tolerate the "free rider," the rough and rowdy protester who contributes to the commotion just for sport. Not a true dissident in any sense of the term, he or she holds no ideological commitment to any oppositional cause, but primarily finds entertainment in the vulgarity of uncivil disobedience. Consider one such view:

> *Steven Green*: "Fun to be vulgar? I'm thinking of the 1999 WTO protests in Seattle. My sense is that there were individuals or groups involved that were not environmentally committed; and they weren't anarchists in the sense of political opponents to powerful government structures. They were just along for the fun of it, and engaged in uncivil protest. . . . They hadn't

identified or articulated what they thought was wrong. They weren't dissenters."

This observation harkens back to our analysis in the preceding chapter. Recall that one of the central attributes of dissent is that it be an "intentional" criticism of an established order.

Moving along the conceptual spectrum, yet others maintain that civil disobedience might well encompass not only uncivil behavior, but potentially violent action. Our next commentator seems cautiously mindful of that point:

> *Sue Curry Jansen*: "Civil disobedience, particularly non-violent civil disobedience, is probably considered within the acceptable range of dissent by the contemporary American public."

Notice that, while Professor Jansen observes that the best case for civil disobedience being classified as dissent is when it is nonviolent, impliedly she does not rule out the possibility that it might be otherwise. (Of course, as we will see in the next chapter, even the category of violent "dissent" will splinter further still.)

To raise the analytical ante, consider this: some would deny the starting premise that civil disobedience, however defined, can claim the mantel of dissent. In this regard, note what a federal judge and a law professor invite us to ponder:

> *Jon O. Newman*: "There are camps who would view civil disobedience as the road to anarchy, and they believe that society ought not to tolerate any violation of the law. They think it's enough to express contrary views peacefully – speeches, writings, civil protests. They would say, 'If you're doing something

illegal, you're outside the purview of dissent.' In other words, they think civil disobedience ought not to have any legal protection, so could not be classified as dissent."

Nadine Strossen: "Some in the culture would probably draw a distinction, insofar as the term 'dissent' connotes to them legitimate methods and modes of conveying your viewpoint. On the other hand, I don't think most people have thought about it."

Such views hold that civil disobedience is not dissent, but merely an illegal act. Dissent only connotes legitimate modes of conveying oppositional viewpoints. For those who hold such views, change is to be brought about in an open and democratic society by legal means – engaging in peaceful and public debate, petitioning the government for a redress of grievances, exercising the franchise, or, if need be, amending the Constitution. Underlying their perspective is the assumption that legitimate dissent must be peaceful, orderly, and lawful. Accordingly, for them, the four different interpretations of civil disobedience mentioned earlier are of no moment. If there is any conceptual slack here, it concerns their understanding of "law;" that is, their views seem tethered to statutory dictates rather than to broader and more elastic constitutional norms. More is said about this general matter in Chapter 3, as we discuss the topic of violent lawlessness, and in Chapter 5, where we examine the function of the First Amendment in supervising the scope of statutory law and expanding the legitimate domain of dissent.

Having cleared much of the analytical brush, we now stand ready to reconsider the relationship between civil disobedience and dissent. At the outset, we think it is too late in the day to maintain that civil disobedience, however defined, cannot be understood as dissent. Too much in our culture and in our system of law acknowledges otherwise. By that measure, Thoreau's refusal to pay a poll tax or Ali's refusal to submit to the draft would surely constitute dissent, albeit punishable under law.

As for the gradations of civil disobedience that we have discussed, we come to a dichotomy. On the one hand, it seems doubtful to us that the Thoreauvian notion of civil disobedience, if left unrestrained, would categorically qualify as dissent, if only because it might include activities such as assassination and terrorism. We will offer our reasons for thinking so later. On the other hand, it seems equally doubtful to us that civil disobedience can be confined to the dictates of propriety, if only because Emily Post's rules of etiquette carry little weight in our contemporary culture. Additionally, we are guardedly open to the notion that certain forms of violence in particular contexts might be said to be dissent – but that discussion must be held in abeyance. For now, we have other matters to contemplate.

ଓ ଛ

In light of our examples and discussion of civil and uncivil disobedience, it is now useful to inquire what attributes may enable us to recognize these forms of disobedience as dissenting activities. Beyond the three key characteristics identified in Chapter I (intentional / public / criticism), are there others that would likely be considered important, either logically or linguistically, when we conceptualize or speak of civil or uncivil disobedience as forms of dissent? Moreover, however central these attributes are in the context of civil or uncivil disobedience, will their presence in other contexts always contribute to our identification of them as modes of dissent?

To answer these questions, we need to explore three additional attributes that can be understood in abbreviated form as follows:

1. *Action:* activism or engagement in a demonstrative and tactically chosen fashion that goes beyond verbal or written criticism (as the latter term was discussed and evaluated in Chapter I).
2. *In-Group Opposition:* membership within the authority structure that is being opposed by criticism or action.
3. *Transgression with a Risk of Sanction or Retribution:* a violation or infringement of a law, policy, practice, or position established by an authority structure, whether legal, religious, scientific, social, or cultural, accompanied by a realistic possibility of incurring governmental punishment or societal obloquy, with its attendant burdens of a substantial character, whether economic or noneconomic, physical or nonphysical.

We now elaborate on each of these attributes.

ACTION

When we speak of dissent, we often refer to actions that people take:

- "The draft-card burners protested against the war."
- "The marchers rallied against abortion."
- "The picketers targeted Walmart for its purported discrimination against women."
- "The demonstrators blocked the doors of Google's headquarters in response to charges of violating the privacy rights of their Internet users."

In these instances and others, dissent goes actively into society in the hope of changing it. This idea is reflected in the way we often refer to dissidents as "activists." As Todd Gitlin puts it, activism pushes dissent "into the world, in a demonstrative and strategically and tactically chosen fashion." At the very least, action emboldens dissent by driving it out of the marketplace of ideas and into the arena of human conflict. For example, in September 1989, members of ACT-UP infiltrated the New York Stock Exchange and protested the exorbitant cost of AZT, the anti-AIDS drug, by chaining themselves to the balconies of the VIPs. And years earlier, in March 1965, César Chávez marched with farmworkers from Delano to Sacramento, California, in protest of California grape growers' labor practices.

When dissent is aligned with action, it moves beyond oral and written advocacy. It involves more than a protest song (e.g., Steve Earl's "Rich Man's War"), a political tract (e.g., Dr. King's public "Letter from a Birmingham Jail"), or a petition for a ballot measure (e.g., the antigay "Protect Marriage Washington" petition). Assuredly, dissent divorced from action can nonetheless be effective, as were Tom Paine's pamphlets or Betty Friedan's *The Feminist*

Mystique. What all of this indicates is that, while action beyond mere criticism is not a sine qua non attribute for dissent, it is regularly linked with it.

The same can be said about civil disobedience as a form of dissent. Although civil disobedience is frequently tied to action beyond criticism, that is not necessarily the case. When in 1918 Eugene Debs forcefully spoke to a crowd of more than 1,000 people in Nimissila Park in Canton, Ohio, he lambasted America's war with Germany; for that, he was arrested and convicted under the Sedition and Espionage Acts for willfully interfering with conscription. For another example, recall Muhammad Ali's conscientious inaction, his refusal of military induction. Of course, as we move from civil to uncivil disobedience, action beyond criticism becomes a likely component.

As action is mixed with other attributes of dissent, civil and uncivil disobedience come into bold relief. Thus, to sharpen our focus, we now turn to such an attribute.

IN-GROUP OPPOSITION

There is, in law, a concept called "standing," which focuses on whether the plaintiff in a lawsuit is the "real party in interest" to bring a case. At a general level, the issue is whether the party has enough of a personal stake in the controversy to sue. In a sense, the attribute of "in-group opposition" is conceptually similar for the phenomenon of dissent. The question is whether an individual has sufficient "standing" within the authority structure that he or she is criticizing to be truly considered a dissenter. Phrased differently, is the individual closely enough aligned with the group, as a member, affiliate, or ally? Does the individual hold enough of a personal stake in the affairs of the association, society, or polity that he or she will likely be viewed as a dissident when intentionally and publicly opposing a law, policy, or norm? By this measure, if a person lacks "standing" – that is, if he or she is outside of the group of interested parties – then there might be no warrant to label that person's critique as dissent.

To illustrate our point, consider this hypothetical: In 2009, Bill Ford, an ordinary U.S. citizen, openly challenges the human rights practices of the Supreme Leader of North Korea, Kim Jong-il, in a public speech that Ford delivers in Olathe, Kansas. Ford's view is shared by the vast majority of his fellow citizens; by contrast, North Koreans would typically believe otherwise. Were Ford in North Korea, or were he a citizen of that nation, his protest might well land him in prison. If he is a dissenter, whether an American or a North Korean, while he is on foreign soil, is he similarly a dissenter when he speaks as an American on U.S. soil?

The idea of in-group opposition would hold that Mr. Ford's comments in the United States disqualify him as a dissenter. After all, he is not a member of the North Korean polity; he has no direct stake in its governance; he is not at any real risk of adverse consequences given the beliefs of his fellow countrymen; and nothing that he says is likely to be effective abroad. He is simply an outlier who disagrees with foreign policy. Put another way, he is not within the zone of the affected group – that is, the "real parties in interest." By this logic, however we label his comments, they could not be branded as dissent.

At first blush, the notion of in-group opposition would seem to be both self-evident and key to any conception of dissent. This is the position taken by the following commentators:

> *Frederick Schauer:* "The essence of dissent is in-group disagreement – disagreement with an opinion that's reached by a group of which you are a part."

> *Randy Barnett:* "I think Fred makes a good point. Dissenters are those within the society. It would be difficult, I think, to say that my disagreement with the Russian government or the Cuban government is dissenting from those governments."

> *Steven Green:* "Dissent does presuppose a relationship with the governmental structure or societal structure. I think there needs to be some sense of connection that an individual must have. Take, for example, the nineteenth-century battles between Protestants and Catholics involving Vatican I in 1870, which declared the pope infallible. Notwithstanding that the Protestants would never consider themselves to be Catholic, they nonetheless considered themselves more broadly as part of the Christian community, and what the pope was doing was offensive to them, and they were therefore dissenting from his claim of infallibility."

The analytical drift of Green's argument is that for the purpose of defining dissent, the sectarian differences between Protestants and Catholics were not determinative. They were nonetheless all part of the Christian community, which is seen by Professor Green as the relevant group. Accordingly, because the Protestants' objections constituted in-group opposition, it counted as dissent.

One might suspect that this move from one level of abstraction to another represents something akin to a conceptual sleight of hand. That is, why is the circle for in-group opposition to the pope's infallibility to be drawn further out at the level of Christians rather than closer in at the level of Catholics? Our next commentator is attentive to this general problem:

> *Steven Shiffrin*: "Imagine Jews criticizing Protestants in the 1940s. America then had a Protestant majority. Jews were not a part of that group; they were a minority. It seems to me their criticism is dissent."

But why would we label such Jewish criticism as dissent? If one were to follow Professor Green's thinking, Jews were not members of the larger Christian community, and thus their protest could not rise to the level of dissent. Then again, expanding on Green's conceptual move, one might respond that the definitional circle should be enlarged to encompass all traditional American religions, including Judaism. But this might prove too much; it simply compounds the sleight-of-hand problem by further abstracting the "in-group" definition.

Unwilling to play this intellectual game, Professor Shiffrin altogether challenges the essentiality of the "in-group opposition" attribute. While he concedes that "the standing of an individual within a group does give the person in many circumstances more credibility as a dissenter," he nevertheless denies that the in-group membership distinction holds merit: "I don't make that distinction." While we are inclined to agree with this view, the matter seems to require a more nuanced response.

On the one hand, as our North Korean hypothetical evidences, there will be contexts in which the principle of in-group opposition would seem a propos. While logically Mr. Ford's intentional and public criticism might be considered dissent, linguistically that smacks of a quantum leap. That is, in light of the facts presented earlier, few if any would likely call Mr. Ford a dissenter.

On the other hand, as our Protestant-Catholic-Jewish scenario evidences, there will be yet other contexts in which the principle of in-group opposition would seem indeterminate. Its very malleability betrays its utility. When classification hinges on manipulating the level of abstraction for the definition of a group, that process becomes so suspect as to undermine the value of the attribute.

All of this notwithstanding, something is to be said in defense of the in-group opposition attribute. Even if we question its centrality, it is hard to deny that the source of opposition can make a salient difference to the appreciation of dissent. In-group opposition stands to make dissent more effective, more poignant, and more risky. That is, the narrower the in-group circle, the more dynamic and dangerous is dissent that comes from within that circle.

Precisely because the risk of punishment or sanction is more probable for those inside a narrower circle than for those outside of it, we wonder whether the attribute of in-group opposition is not better understood as a proxy for proof of other attributes, with which it works in tandem. That brings us to consideration of our next set of attributes.

TRANSGRESSION WITH A RISK OF SANCTION OR RETRIBUTION

There is a comic adage that goes: "Tell your boss what you think of him, and the truth will set you free." Indeed, speaking truth to power can, and often does, have its consequences. Here, assuming no issue of insubordination, our hypothetical free-speaking employee – call her Nancy Jones – has clearly engaged in criticism that is risky, but has not transgressed any law or norm. Her coworkers might well see her candor about the indifference of her boss, Steve Roberts, to the dangerous working conditions in the plant as her admirable declaration of dissent.

Notably, this example brings dissent into the *private* sphere, where open criticism is directed against private individuals or entities. While we are abundantly comfortable with the idea of dissent being directed against the government, we may hesitate a bit when it is directed against private actors. Let us now test whether or how much of a difference that might make.

To continue our hypothetical, if Mr. Roberts were of liberal persuasion and believed in freedom of speech within the workplace, he might not discipline or fire his critic. Of course, that would not change the fact that Ms. Jones's original complaint against him was a form of dissent. And that still would be the case if she knew beforehand that her boss would not punish her. In other words, dissent may or may not involve a transgression and it may or may not involve some kind of risk (as the example of judicial dissent in Chapter I surely illustrates).

Let us now assume that after Ms. Jones was critical of her boss and Mr. Roberts did not retaliate, he nonetheless discounted the merits of her criticism. That is, he heard her criticism and elected to do nothing. Outraged by her employer's inaction, she takes her dissent a step further. Ms. Jones knowingly and maliciously spreads false rumors about Mr. Roberts, alleging that he gave bribes to secure governmental contracts. Unsatisfied with committing only defamation, Ms. Jones thereafter ratchets up her "dissent" by intentionally destroying company property. In both instances, she is willing to accept the consequences of her actions.

Let us begin with Ms. Jones's slander: Can such defamation be dissent? It is surely a transgression, for it is a civil wrong, which has legal consequences. Were the same malicious defamation directed instead at a government official, it would likely be designated as dissent, even though it would, strictly speaking, be unprotected speech. So, are these two forms of defamation different? If the latter is dissent, would not the same hold true for the former? Perhaps, yes; then again, we might say that such defamation is not dissent, at least when the only intended objective is to harm a private individual and not to criticize him. But if that were the case, why wouldn't the same hold true for the government official?

We turn next to Ms. Jones's destruction of company property. Can it also constitute dissent? Although a fuller discussion of the relationship between dissent and violent action is reserved for our next chapter, suffice it to say here that crimes against property may, in certain contexts, be deemed dissent. For our purposes, that proposition has valence because it reveals that intentional injuries of private rights may hover under the umbrella of dissent. And if, in this case, the violation of a property right rises to a level of dissent, then by the same token should not the infringement of a reputational right be treated likewise?

This discussion sets the stage for our examination of the attributes of transgression and the risk of sanction or retribution. Consider this correlation: the greater the transgression, the greater the risk of consequences; and the greater the risk of consequences, the greater the likelihood of labeling something as dissent, at least generally speaking. Let us now tease this out.

Harry Cohen is a practicing Jew, but not always observant. Sometimes he takes liberties; he eats pork. Harry knows that such dietary behavior runs counter to the longstanding norms of his religion. But Harry loves bacon sandwiches, and occasionally indulges himself. Predictably, he is challenged by his Jewish friends, and always responds by criticizing the prohibition as long outliving its original purpose. Even so, no one in his circle gets too worked up about this, and they tolerate his culinary breaches and his continued disrespect for Jewish law.

Is Mr. Cohen a religious dissenter? Unquestionably, he has transgressed and criticized a deeply entrenched norm of his faith community. Does it make any difference that there are no real risks of adverse consequences? Does his colleagues' toleration disqualify his actions as dissent? Logically analyzed, his conduct passes muster under the key attributes of dissent – it is intentional and public criticism of a well-established norm. Linguistically analyzed, however, few would tag Harry as a religious dissenter. His criticism seems suspect, if only because it is self-serving in the sense that it may only be a way of rationalizing his food preferences. Moreover, the absence of any meaningful consequences, though not logically determinative of his status, suggests that Harry is a more of a dietary dilettante than a religious dissenter.

Fate being what it is, however, one day Harry finds himself the object of considerable obloquy in his Jewish community. Among others, his rabbi castigates him openly for his flagrant disrespect of Jewish doctrine. Unwilling to yield, Harry launches a "Jews for Pork" campaign, hoping to highlight what he views as the absurdity of such norms. As a result, Harry becomes a pariah in his community and is shunned by many of his Jewish friends. Even his wife and children take strong exception to what they consider a silly and offensive cause, akin to the sort of "stupid" thing expected from the clueless character, Larry David, of *Curb Your Enthusiasm* television fame.

With these facts, we are more likely to label Mr. Cohen's actions as dissent, primarily because the consequences are far greater. Such consequences suggest that there is more than taste or simple disagreement at stake here; there is an intentional violation of a norm that results in a social stigma, in Harry's marginalization within his community.

Remember: Mr. Cohen broke no law of the state. Rather, he transgressed a religious norm. And as the ramifications of his conduct became more severe, and when thereafter he continued to act in an openly critical manner, the result is that we are more likely to see him as an outcast, as a bona fide dissenter. Hence, while the transgression of a norm or law coupled with a risk of negative consequences is not essential to the definition of dissent, it is nonetheless a clear sign of its existence.

By contrast, for the kinds of dissent explored in this chapter – civil and uncivil disobedience – transgression and risk of punishment are both formally and functionally essential. To illustrate, assume that Harry lived in country where the dietary norms were also mandated by the state. In that instance, if his unlawful actions were intended to criticize such policies, he would surely be deemed a civil disobedient and, of course, a dissenter.

ᘓ ᘔ

As we have seen, by first coming to understand the character of civil and uncivil disobedience, we become more clear-minded about the general phenomenon of dissent. Difficult as that exercise is, to proceed without it would produce a false confidence about our inquiry, while at the same time leaving many conceptual problems unresolved. In light of that, we were better prepared to reflect on three more attributes of dissent, namely action, in-group opposition, and transgression with a risk of sanction or retribution. Although these attributes do not always lie at the conceptual and linguistic core of dissent, when they are present in an expression or action, it increases the probability of naming it dissent. To be sure, more needs to be said. There are still other candidates for dissent to consider, along with other attributes relevant to our general subject.

CHAPTER III

THE VAGARIES OF VIOLENCE

Violence is a loaded word. Its use often dictates the direction of thought. While noble objectives may sometimes legitimate violence, by the same token violence may sometimes delegitimate those goals. The caché of any ideal may be placed in jeopardy by its mere association with violence. Only consider the phrase "Reign of Terror." In many minds, that is enough to undercut the ostensibly justifiable aims of even an egalitarian revolt, such as the French Revolution of 1789.

Clearly, there is something unsettling about the specter of violence and language that validates it. This is especially true in the context of dissent. For when it runs in tandem with violence, dissent may all too easily be severed from its definitional moorings. This is not, however, to deny that there may be a place for violence in the conceptual cabin of dissent. It is only to stress the importance of proceeding with caution.

Let us continue, if only for the purpose of utility, with the *Oxford English Dictionary* definition of "violence." At a high level of abstraction, violence is characterized as "the exercise of physical force so as to cause injury or damage to a person or property." Not surprisingly, what this explanation elides are gradations of harm; definitionally, it is as though all violence is created equal. But such cannot be the case for any sober and profound understanding of dissent. Whether violent conduct is likely to be considered an act of dissent may depend on its placement in the full spectrum of violence, running from petty damage to property and minor injury to person on the one end to terrorism and assassination on the other end.

Here, perhaps more so than in the previous chapters, the need to align the notion of dissent with its essential attributes (intentional / public / criticism) is particularly important. Otherwise, any valid notion of dissent may unravel to the point of irrelevancy. Even if all the attributes of dissent are present in a violent scenario, however, it may still fail to be termed dissent. For there is, roughly speaking, a reverse proportionality between the quantity and quality of violence associated with conduct and our willingness to label that conduct as dissent. While this may not always be a logical imperative, it may nonetheless be a linguistic one. That is, although the mind might embrace the notion that assassination can be synonymous with dissent, the tongue strains to speak in that vernacular. For example, how many of us would call Leon Czolgosz's 1901 murder of President William McKinley an act of dissent?

Mindful of these considerations, we now turn to the world of violence.

ભ છ૭

May 17, 1968: On that Friday afternoon, nine Catholic antiwar activists stormed into a Selective Service office in Cantonsville, Maryland. Proceeding past shocked employees,
Philip Berrigan and his eight pacifist cohorts pilfered 600
draft records from file cabinets and piled them into two
wire baskets. They then dumped the records in an adjacent
parking lot and set them on fire with homemade napalm.
Holding hands and circling around the flames, they vociferously recited The Lord's Prayer. The local press, which
the protestors had alerted in advance, filmed and reported
on the spectacle. According to Anne Klejmant, "[f]or Philip
Berrigan, who convinced the group of its value, property
destruction was hardly an innovative tactic. Harkening back
to the example of the Boston Tea Party, he viewed the raid
as another action in the American revolutionary tradition."
Five months later, the Cantonsville Nine were sentenced to
eighteen years in prison.

January 26, 2010: Emily McCoy, a New York City member
of People for the Ethical Treatment of Animals (PETA),
aimed to express her outrage over the Canadian government's support of seal hunting. As the Fisheries and Oceans
Minister Gail Shea delivered a speech at the opening of the
Aquatic Life Research Facility in Burlington, Canada, the
PETA protestor shoved a tofu cream pie into the face of
the Prince Edward Island Member of Parliament, bellowing
"Shame on you, Gail Shea. It is a shame on Canada that she
has not denounced this bloody seal hunt." Although Shea
did not need medical attention and retook the podium after
cleaning her face, McCoy was arrested and charged with

assault and battery. After PETA assumed responsibility in a press release announcing that the incident was part of its campaign "to stop the government's ill-advised sanction of the slaughter of seals," Liberal MP Gerry Byrne called on the government to investigate whether PETA acted as a terrorist organization under Canadian law. PETA's executive vice-president, Tracy Reiman, tried to put things in calmer perspective: "A little tofu pie on her face is hardly comparable to the blood on Ms. Shea's hands."

Might we think of this ceremonial act of property destruction and this practice of battery by pieing as forms of dissent? Both examples satisfy the key elements of dissent, insofar as they represent intentional actions to publicly criticize government policies. But both examples also satisfy the dictionary definition of violence. That raises the issue of whether and when violent behavior can be deemed dissent.

For some, the presence of violence is categorically determinative; its manifestation *per force* disqualifies an act from being dignified as dissent:

> *Ralph Nader:* "The line between dissent and violence is clear. Violence cannot be called dissent. It has to be called violence."

If Mr. Nader confines the compass of dissent, he does so in the interest of preserving its rhetorical currency. For him, dissent has a venerable connotation. Although we might disagree with a dissenting act, there is something honorable about it. His fear is that if dissent keeps the company of violence, it will soon enough be viewed as dishonorable. "I think violence is a huge boomerang," Nader added. The danger of lumping peaceful protest together with violent confrontation is the problem of push-back – soon enough, society becomes unsympathetic and intolerant of anything branded dissent. "Thus, dissent needs a definitional barrier. Once you don't draw that line," Nader continued, "dissent loses its historic and constitutional caché." The lesson that Mr. Nader implores us to learn is that labels matter. What dissent gains in the name of elasticity it stands to lose in the name of credibility – or so the argument goes.

Were Mr. Nader to hold steadfast to his position, he would be compelled to remove the Berrigan and McCoy violence from the purview of dissent. But, when tested, he does not hold steadfast. In such instances, his absolutism becomes qualified. Exploits such as those of Berrigan and McCoy "have value if they're willing to be open about it and take the consequences," Nader emphasized. By this qualification, he saves himself from denying what most would concede – that these acts of protest are forms of dissent. But by this qualification, he loses the clarity of his bright-line thinking: no longer is violence definitionally barred from an understanding of dissent.

More problematic is the return of Mr. Nader's boomerang problem. If all it takes to move violence to the mantel of dissent is the openness of action and willingness to assume legal responsibility, then even the assassin's deeds would constitute dissent if they fulfill these conditions. Of course, Nader would not countenance this possibility, which means that his understanding of dissent would require greater qualification. We suspect that what he intends *sub silentio* is to buttress his position with some accounting for gradations of violence.

For now, what our discussion reveals is that violence directed either at property or persons need not automatically be excluded from how we think about dissent. There will be instances, as our two examples reveal, where such violence does not seriously impugn the integrity of dissent. Then again, there will be other instances where the character of violence is so egregious as to trump any meaningful paradigm for dissent. Either way, what is important is that there be some principle of gradation – some assessment of the degrees of violence and their relationship to a viable understanding of dissent. More will be said about this after we entertain extreme examples of violence and the views of those who would be willing to call them dissenting activities.

ᙅ ᙍ

April 14, 1865: At Ford's Theater in Washington, DC, President Abraham Lincoln sat with his wife, Mary, and two friends, Miss Clara Harris and Major Henry Rathbone, to take in Laura Keene's *Our American Cousin*. The fifty-six-year old Confederate sympathizer, John Wilkes Booth, armed with a single-shot Deringer pistol and a large Rio Grande Camp Knife, made his way to the president's box at approximately 10:10 PM. Booth took aim, and a shot rang out. The .44-caliber ball pierced Lincoln's head on the lower-left side, a little below the ear, coming to rest in his brain, lodged behind his right eye. Major Rathbone rose from his seat and lunged for Booth, grabbing at his coat. Crying "Freedom," Booth aimed the knife at Rathbone's heart, but struck his upper arm when the Major parried the thrust. Turning to the balustrade, Booth climbed out of the box to leap below. When one of his spurs snagged on a flag, he hit the stage unevenly, fracturing his left leg. Moving painfully to center stage, Booth stood proudly erect, paused for dramatic effect, held his bloody dagger high in the air, and bellowed, "*Sic semper tyrannis!* ("Thus always to tyrants!") The South is avenged!" Fleeing off stage right and rushing through the wings, he exited the theater's back door to the alley where his bay mare awaited his escape. The president died in a brick rowhouse on Tenth Street across from the theater the next day, April 15, at 7:22 AM. Eleven days later, Booth was captured at the Garrett farm in Virginia, where he was fatally wounded in the neck.

April 3, 1996: Federal agents seized Theodore Kaczynski (a.k.a., "The Unabomber") at a remote cabin in the woods of Lincoln, Montana. The Harvard-educated former assistant professor of mathematics at UC-Berkeley was a modern-day Luddite who railed against the industrial-technological system. Over the course of eighteen years, he mailed letter-bombs or hand-delivered explosive packages to computer science professors, researchers at high-tech companies, advertising executives, and industry lobbyists, among others. Before the authorities caught up with him, his deadly handiwork had killed three people and injured twenty-three. To disseminate his radical views, he tendered "The Unabomber Manifesto" to several mainstream newspapers that published it. Kaczynski's militant tract declared: "The Industrial Revolution and its consequences have been a disaster for the human race.... The industrial-technological system [can only survive] at the cost of permanently reducing human beings and many other living organisms to engineered products and mere cogs in the social machine." He concluded: "We therefore advocate a revolution against the industrial system." In an interview three years later, Kaczynski further explained his motivation: "I got involved in political issues because I was driven to it. . . . I don't think there is any controlled or planned way in which we can dismantle the industrial system. I think the only way we will get rid of it is if it breaks down and collapses. . . . The real revolutionaries should separate themselves from the reformers." Kaczynski's criminal acts culminated in a life sentence without the possibility of parole.

What are we to make of these examples? Can they also be placed under the umbrella of dissent? After all, they satisfy the core attributes for dissenting activity: Booth and Kaczynski both intended their acts to be public and critical of the prevailing authorities and orthodoxies. And, as we just discussed, if violence against a person does not necessarily disqualify an act as dissenting, then Booth's and Kaczynski's ventures might be candidates for dissent. Obviously, these examples present physical harms of a far more severe order than Ms. McCoy's pie-throwing. Does that make a difference? And, if so, why?

Some hold that differences in the degree of harm are of no conceptual significance:

Steven Shiffrin: "Violent confrontation, property damage, arson, looting, physical battery, rock throwing, punching or clubbing, imminent incitements to riot or revolution, assassination, and terrorism . . . would certainly be disapproved in our culture in most contexts . . . or would not be regarded as dissent, but just regarded as criminal activity. Personally, I regard all of these as dissent, because they are all methods of criticizing existing customs, institutions, habits, and authorities. I do not regard dissent as absolutely good or bad."

For Professor Shiffrin, then, it appears sufficient to brand an act as dissent once it has crossed his definitional threshold. His evaluation does not turn on any analysis of the gradations of violence, because he does not insist on any positive connotation for dissent. This concession would surely disturb the likes of Ralph Nader, who would understand Shiffrin's position as altogether abrogating any rhetorical power for dissent.

Professor Shiffrin might counter that what *really* matters is not the expansive scope of the meaning of dissent, but rather how the law would treat it. Apparently, what Shiffrin most cares about is whether the First Amendment can be recruited in the service of this or that dissenting act. It is on that plane that he calibrates the degrees of violence: "I don't think that arson or looting or physical battery or rock-throwing . . . incitements to riot or revolution, or terrorism are ever protected by the First Amendment, or should be." By contrast, he would extend legal protection to certain less violent forms of dissent. Thus, for him, concerns such as Nader's are more academic than pragmatic.

We respectfully dissent. We discern something troubling in Professor Shiffrin's "pragmatic" stance. It is not pragmatic enough. Clearly, Professor Shiffrin does not believe that the concept of dissent needs to do much conceptual spadework; that is to be left to statutory and constitutional law. But the law, as legal realists know all too well, does not operate in a vacuum; it is both a mirror and a mold of how Americans think, speak, and act. As our Prologue explained at some length, there is much cultural spadework to be done in the field of dissent before the law comes onto the scene to grant or deny its protection.

For example, if a significant quotient of the culture had not perceived and appreciated the character of dissent inherent in the African-American demonstrations and sit-ins of the 1960s or in the newspaper condemnations of Southern intransigence to the civil rights movement, then rights-affirming Supreme Court decisions such as *Griffin v. Maryland*, *NAACP v. Claiborne Hardware Company*, or *New York Times v. Sullivan* would not likely have issued. Moreover, if the law is sometimes leniently applied to the robust and unruly demonstrations of the Occupy Wall Street movement, can it reasonably be claimed that police, prosecutors, and judges are blind to the element of bona fide dissent integral to those protests? By the same token, if juries sometimes refuse to convict protestors charged with a violent crime, can we reasonably believe that their verdicts were altogether uninfluenced by any respect for the dissenting activity?

We grant, of course, that the criminal and civil violations in these cases cannot compare to our examples of assassination and terrorism. But if the law does not protect such extreme violence as dissent, it is because the culture will not validate them as dissent. In hesitating to distinguish among forms of dissent, Professor Shiffrin focuses more on the results of legal decision making than on the cultural processes that produced them.

CR SO

In our enthusiasm to engage Professor Shiffrin, we did not squarely address the soundness of the claim that assassination and terrorism might be understood as forms of dissent, at least in certain instances. If some are hesitant to go that far, why are they so? If others go there, how do they justify doing so? Some commentators are loath to dignify criminal conduct, such as that of John Wilkes Booth, Theodore Kaczynski, and other extremely violent actors, with the badge of dissent:

> *Michael Walzer:* "John Wilke Booth's assassination of Abraham Lincoln was not an act of dissent, but an act of murder. It may have been motivated by dissent, but I want to confine and describe dissent as political, intellectual engagement with one's fellow citizens. And violence, insurrection, revolution, terrorism – these are not intellectual, political engagements. They're military engagements. They are of a different sort."

For Mr. Walzer, the editor of *Dissent* magazine, the understanding of dissent hinges on the difference between civic engagement and military engagement. The former aims to persuade, whereas the latter aims to coerce. The former yearns to be dialogic; the latter insists on being destructive. Finally, the former works to reform the established order, while the latter hopes to topple it. In all of these ways, noble aspirations inform the meaning of dissent. Similar thinking animates the perspective of another commentator:

> *Nadine Strossen:* "I do think the word 'dissent' has a positive connotation. It tries to persuade; it has that connotation rather

than using coercion. The line is often not bright between the two. But extreme cases of severe violence against person or property fall clearly on the other side of the persuasion-versus-coercion line."

For both Walzer and Strossen, then, the ideal of dissent is linked to a worthy tradition, a proud heritage of civic criticism dating back centuries in Western history. In this respect, dissent in its pristine form reflects the noblest mores of the people and calls them to be morally engaged. This point is made eloquently by the next commentator:

> *Howard Zinn*: "While obviously revolution, assassination, and terrorism are anti-establishment, anti-government, anti-norm, I think it distorts the meaning of dissent to bring those actions within it – like the planting of bombs, the willingness to 'off the pigs.' I do not include those in the parameters of dissent, because I want to make moral distinctions among forms of dissent."

To coin a phrase, we might think of such arguments in terms of *the morality of dissent*. If this morality circumscribes the parameters of dissent, it does so to foster respect for it, even when it is unlawful. But this conception cannot at one and the same time take the moral high ground while descending to the depths of unrestrained violence.

The proceeding arguments prompt us to consider whether there are credible arguments in defense of a conceptual haven for assassination and terrorism in the curtilage of dissent. While it may be difficult to speak of extreme violence as dissent, for now our attention focuses on the analytical compatibility of the two. The following comment by Professor Geoffrey Stone presents a perspective that, at first blush, seems akin to that advanced by Mr. Walzer. Yet when scrutinized, it is of an entirely different order. First, Stone distinguishes between intellectual versus military engagements, as does Walzer, but on the basis of an actor's open and intentional criticism. Second, Stone concedes the possibility that in certain instances extreme violence may constitute dissent. Insofar as Stone's argument goes, it provides a bridge between those who would deny dissenting status to assassination or terrorism and those who might qualifiedly grant it. Having said that, we now allow our commentator to speak for himself:

> *Geoffrey Stone*: "To the extent that you're doing violence for the sake of preventing troop trains from getting to a war or you're killing the President in order to stop a war, then that's not intended to express criticism. That's an act designed to prevent something from happening. Acts of preventing the government from functioning may arise out of the same beliefs as dissent, but wouldn't fit within my understanding of dissent, because the intent is not to express criticism, it's to subvert the government from acting. Of course, you'll have multiple motives in many actions. But if you assume we're talking about black and white intents here, then it seems to me that the same act can have different intents."

In a noteworthy way, then, Professor Stone aligns himself with the likes of Strossen, Walzer, and Zinn. He, too, declines to classify coercive militant acts as dissent, at least when they aim primarily at obstructing governmental functions. Resting on the three key attributes of intention, public, and criticism for dissent, his definitional argument sometimes comes to the same result as those who look to the gradations of harm and the morality of dissent to exclude assassination and terrorism. Insofar as it has the same effect, Stone's position strengthens the positive connotations and rhetorical currency traditionally accorded to the concept of dissent.

Notably, however, Professor Stone also breaks away from the camp of Strossen, Walzer, and Zinn. He is willing, within certain contexts and under certain conditions, to maintain that extreme violence is dissent. That is, if assassination and terrorism are openly intended to express criticism, Stone would include extreme cases of violence such as those of Booth and Kaczynski within the category of dissent. Concurring in that judgment, the following commentator makes a similar point:

> *Steven Green*: "John Wilkes Booth was both a criminal and a dissenter. He was pro-slavery and supported the Southern cause. He identified Lincoln as being a tyrant, as being someone who had taken on powers that were inappropriate and had been misused. And so, to me, it seems like he was expressing some form of dissent."

In a significant respect, Professors Stone and Green are willing to keep Shiffrin's company, and expect statutory and constitutional law to do the work of distinguishing between legitimate and illegitimate dissent. Implicitly, concerns about the positive connotations of dissent fall by the wayside. Seen in this light, Professors Stone and Green's perspectives have a Janus-like quality: they gaze in both directions to bridge those who would deny and those who would affirm the dissenting status for violent acts.

CR SO

We are sympathetic, in a general sense, with those who stressed what we coined as the morality of dissent. Like them, we understand that, at some point, degrees of violence taint the purity of persuasive exercise that is a primary hallmark of dissent. That is, the more that violence is poured into the beaker of dissent, the more it dilutes its staying power. This is particularly the case in a democratic and free-speech culture such as our own, which furnishes many nonviolent avenues for opposition to governmental policies and practices. Moreover, that same culture, at least in its finer moments, tolerates both civil and uncivil protest. Contrast that with the rule of much more tyrannical and oppressive regimes, in which violent dissent takes on a different connotation because of its necessity and efficacy.

Notwithstanding these sympathies, we cannot abide the notion that there is no room whatsoever for any violence, however minor, in the conceptual realm of dissent. For us, the draft-records burning of the Cantonsville Nine and the pie-throwing of PETA's protestor are assuredly dissenting activities, both logically and linguistically speaking. Not only do these cases satisfy the essential attributes of dissent, but they clearly fall at the more inconsequential end of the spectrum of violence. Assessed relatively, these scenarios involve minor destruction of property and slight physical injury to person. While we might not condone them, we are willing nonetheless to endorse them as forms of dissent, albeit illegal. Furthermore, as we already suggested, we posit that our language usage would confirm this point. We even concede that, in particular contexts, a meaningful notion of dissent can move further along the spectrum to more serious gradations of harm.

Many, including us, would see a line – not hard-and-fast, but decipherable – between injury to property and to person. To the extent that harm to property is connected, both contextually and symbolically, to a greater ideological objective, it may still deserve the name of dissent, provided it does not tend to the extreme. Consider, for example, the following hypothetical: A devout Evangelical drives her car through the front door of an abortion clinic after closing with the intent to publicize her outrage over "the murder of innocents." In that the protestor's conduct has a purposeful nexus to intentional public criticism of abortion, it stands to share some of the luster of dissent. That luster would fade, however, were the protestor to ratchet up the violence by bombing the clinic, even if no one were injured. We are loath to label this act dissent for at least two reasons: the property damage is catastrophic; and more importantly, bombings are inherently dangerous given the foreseeable likelihood of loss of life or limb.

To the extent that harm to property is not connected to any greater ideological objective, or is simply violence for violence's sake, then it should not be billed dissent, either logically or linguistically. That is, few would call mere hooliganism a form of dissent. For example, if teenagers on a vandalism spree hurl rocks through the windows of an abortion clinic, no one would dignify their actions with the name of dissent. This illustrates an extremely important consideration in our analysis of the relationship between violence and dissent. No matter where a violent act falls along the spectrum of gradated harm, if that action does not satisfy the key attributes for dissent, it is disqualified at the outset.

This same point holds constant whether the harm is to property or person. Take, for instance, the assassination of John Lennon. When in 1980 Mark David Chapman fired five hollow-point bullets into Lennon as he walked into the doors of the Dakota, did his assassin's act qualify as dissent? Admittedly, Lennon's songs "God" and "Imagine" bothered Chapman, and he was troubled by what he perceived as the hypocrisy of the singer's lifestyle when compared to the songs he wrote, but was that enough to place the cloak of dissent on Chapman's violence? We think not. Chapman's behavior was more that of a deranged man than that of a heroic dissident. His desire for notoriety, if that is what it was, precluded him from being a dissenter if only because he never expressed an intention to criticize an authority figure. This example reinforces the lesson that certain acts, whether mildly or extremely violent, may fail as dissent because they lack its core attributes. When that is so, there is no need to consider the gradation of violence involved. Professor Geoffrey Stone makes the point well: "Dissent turns on the intention of the actor." It is a simple maxim that must always be kept in mind.

To move further along the spectrum, there are many forms of extreme violence – including revolution, assassination, and terrorism – that we might not consider to be modes of dissent, even as a logical matter, because they cannot easily be reconciled with the attribute of in-group opposition, which we discussed in Chapter 2. To illustrate this, let us focus on the phenomenon of revolution. Typically, it is an outgrowth – although an extreme one – of the same beliefs that fuel dissent. But there is a logical difference between the reformer's intentional public criticism and the revolutionary's violent action to subvert the government. The reformer seeks to remain within and preserve the government, whereas the revolutionary stands outside and aims to overthrow it. This argument is supported ably by the following commentator:

> *Frederick Schauer.* "You can be a violent dissenter as well as a non-violent dissenter. Except at some point, violent dissenters cease to be members of the group, and then we don't really think of them as dissenters. Once you take a variety of actions that indicate a desire to leave or totally distance yourself from a group, you're not a dissenter from that group as much as you are no longer in it. We don't think of revolutionaries or terrorists as dissenters. We may think of them as dissenters at the very beginning, but once they become revolutionaries it's odd to think of them as dissenters. Because they don't want to be a member of the group; so they're not dissenting from it, they want to get rid of it."

In other words, the criticism of a dissenter is not analogous to the militant acts of a revolutionary, assassin, or terrorist. While exercises of dissent may, over time, become more robust and blossom into revolution, the dissident makes the journey from insider to outsider, from group member to outlier, from reformer to insurrectionist, and from peaceful and mildly violent acts to forceful and excessively violent acts. In short, the difference is between persuasion on the one hand and coercion on the other.

Moreover, even if a moderately or extremely violent act meets all of the definitional criteria of dissent as a logical matter, we are convinced that, as a linguistic matter, it is not likely to be called dissent, particularly when it crosses the line from property destruction to personal injury. In this regard, consider the following commentators:

> *Sut Jhally*: "Violence can be a public expression of dissent . . . as long as it is directed to property, and not persons. Most people would draw that line – attacking property is different than attacking persons."

> *Nadine Strossen*: "If you're talking about actual, physical harm to human beings, that crosses the boundary. But property crimes do not necessarily cross a boundary that would remove them from a legitimate sphere of dissent."

Put succinctly, persons matter – more so than property. While this may not be categorically so, as our pie-throwing example illustrated, it is nonetheless a culturally determined norm. This is the case even when the violence directed against a person is performed for purportedly noble reasons. Murdering an abortion doctor is unquestionably different than damaging an abortion clinic. Consider the scenario that occurred in March 1993 during an anti-abortion protest in Florida. As he exited his car at the Pensacola Women's Medical Service Clinic, David Gunn, a physician who performed abortions, was shot in the chest several times by Michael Frederick Griffin. Just before the murder, Griffin reportedly said to Gunn, "Don't kill any more babies!" Subsequently, Griffin approached a policeman on the scene of the protest and confessed to the murder. Much in what Griffin did has the indicia of dissent, but the harm principle trumps all of it. However one views abortion, we trust that society is far more likely to speak of Griffin's act as a murderous crime than as honorable dissent. The logic of language suggests that the way we speak reveals the way we think. If so, that we do not speak of murder, assassination, terrorism, or revolution in the language of dissent tells us much – that we do not conceive of them as dissent.

To recapitulate, we might exclude violent behavior from the realm of dissent for at least five reasons. First, the rhetorical currency of dissent is devalued when it is aligned with more extreme forms of violence. Second, it may lack the essential attributes of dissent. Third, moving along the spectrum of harm to property, it may be so severe as to be morally reprehensible. Fourth, harm to persons is far less likely to deserve the title of dissent. And finally, the violence may be so extreme as to indicate that the perpetrator is an outlier who seeks to overthrow the system rather than to reform it.

All this said, we are more willing to cast our lot with the likes of Walzer, Strossen, Zinn, Jhally, and Schauer than with the likes of Nader, Shiffrin, Stone, and Green, although we do not deny that there is a good measure of merit in what they argue. For the reasons first presented in our Prologue and reinforced in our analysis of Shiffrin's expansive understanding of dissent, we strongly maintain that a meaningful notion of dissent can and should do much conceptual spadework – in both logical and linguistic ways – to distinguish among the vagaries of violence that may be understood as bona fide modes of dissent. And although we may differ from Nader in the results of his analysis, we do appreciate the power of his reasoning. We, too, believe that dissent should have a positive connotation in the public realm that might unfortunately be squandered if the concept slums with any form of violence, whatever its quantity or quality.

Finally, given the complex and contextualized relationship between dissent and violence, we believe that any violent act – even the least violent – stands little chance of being conceived or spoken of as dissent if it does not hew closely to most, if not all, of the attributes characteristic of dissent, be they core or beyond. That is, the greater the nexus between a violent enterprise and the complete paradigm for dissent, the greater the probability that it will be understood as a dissenting activity. In this regard, we move to the exploration of two final attributes, which may further assist us in determining whether a violent scenario might be associated with dissent. In other words, there is yet more work to be done.

ଓ ଛ

The final two attributes for our consideration can be understood in abbreviated form as follows:

1. *Relative Powerlessness:* expression or action undertaken by an individual or group with relative political, economic, or social powerlessness vis-à-vis the target of opposition.
2. *Acknowledgment of the Rule of Law and the Acceptance of Punishment*: a knowing willingness to be punished for the violation of laws or cultural norms that are believed to be unconstitutional, unjust, immoral, or otherwise illegitimate.

We now elaborate on both of these attributes.

RELATIVE POWERLESSNESS

They felt alienated from their country, victimized by the status quo, outraged by the tyranny of the legal system, and ignored in all their cries for social change. These were the days of rage, when students across the United States became increasingly confrontational in their opposition to the capitalist, imperialist, warmongering power structure. Discontent was in the air on the afternoon of February 25, 1970, when the radical lawyer, William Kunstler, addressed a crowd of 7,000 who paid 50 cents apiece to hear him speak on the football field of the University of California at Santa Barbara. Almost a week after five of the Chicago Seven were convicted of incitement to riot, their lead counsel denounced the fanaticism of the police state and the oppression of the courts. Stirring up student passion, Kunstler railed: "I think the shadow of the swastika is on every court house, on universities, on government buildings, maybe even on the apartment door next to you." Hours later, an agitated mob of 2,000 pelted the local police with rocks and set a squad car afire in the neighboring student community of Isla Vista. After the police retreated, the rioters advanced to the most prominent symbol of the Establishment in the vicinity, the Bank of America, which had been vandalized the night before.

It was a stark spectacle of violence. With its windows smashed out and its doors broken open, the empty bank was a target for anarchy. The enraged crowd seized the opportunity to push a large burning trash can against the building's draperies. As they heaped cardboard onto the flames, some chanted "Burn, baby, burn!" and "Death to corporations!" When the blaze reached a ruinous pitch, the roof collapsed, and the bank was in time reduced to its shell. In Governor Ronald Reagan's eyes, these were the acts of "cowardly, little bums" who were egged on by Kunstler. The activist lawyer saw things differently: he had not incited the violence, yet he was inclined to understand it. "I never thought that the breaking of windows or sporadic violence is a good tactic," Kunstler declared. "But on the other hand, I cannot bring myself to become bitter and condemn young people who engage in it."

If Kunstler perceived this destruction of property as a form of dissent, it might be because of the political power dynamic between those who opposed the status quo and those empowered to perpetuate it. No doubt, he would have felt the same way about the Cantonsville Nine and their burning of draft card files. Were the mantle of dissent to be laid upon one or both of these activities, it would be due in large part to the attribute of relative powerlessness. Along with the other essential attributes of dissent, this one renders such violent acts as possible candidates for dissent. Even so, relative powerlessness cannot guarantee that such violence would ultimately be deemed dissent.

In one sense, it is obvious: the concept of powerlessness is inherent in the idea of dissent. After all, if one had the power to act as one wished, there would be no need to dissent. One resorts to the latter precisely because one lacks the former. Two of our commentators succinctly make this point:

Martha Nussbaum: "Usually, of course, the reason why you are dissenting is that you are relatively powerless."

Howard Zinn: "The notion of dissent implies that there is a power greater than you against which you are dissenting. You are certainly powerless in relation to the force – whether it's the nation or the church or the corporation – that you're dissenting against."

This is not a simple tautology, however, for relative powerlessness works in tandem with other significant attributes of dissent, such as the risk of sanction or retribution. That is, there is an integral relationship between a lack of power to promote a particular agenda and the prospect of suffering retaliation for doing so. In more common parlance, it is the powerful who punish the powerless, and not vice versa. It is precisely such thinking that gives currency to Kunstler's intimation that the burning of the bank might be viewed as dissent.

In another sense, things are not so obvious: a dissenter may be quite powerful. One may be a person of considerable socioeconomic and political power and still be powerless to prevail over that which one opposes. Assume, for example, that a wealthy and socially prominent shareholder of the Bank of America participated in its fiery destruction because he had come, against all odds, to accept the gospel of violent radicalism. In determining whether the shareholder's participation constitutes dissent, does his eminent status stand to disqualify him? Or consider the example of a powerful Catholic cardinal who openly endorses same-sex marriage in clear contravention of religious dictates. Despite his authoritative position in the church, is the cardinal not a dissenter?

If the shareholder and the cardinal are engaged in dissent because they otherwise satisfy its essential attributes, their status may well serve to ennoble their acts. That is, they stand to be condemned more roundly by their own class and therefore to lose a great deal more than the powerless. The fall of the elevated, of course, is all the harder, and because of that is likely to be viewed as more admirable by their ideological cohorts, as the following commentaries indicate:

> *Sut Jhally*: "You can be at the heart of the power structure and be a dissenter. In fact, I think the more you are, the more powerful the dissent is."

> *Hans Linde:* "Clearly, one can be a dissenter even with significant political or socioeconomic power. That is the dissenter who may well get into trouble. That is the dissenter who is likely to be pursued because he or she is perceived as a threat."

So where does this all leave us? How important is the attribute of relative powerlessness to our understanding of dissent? On the one hand, it is inherent at some level in any notion of dissent. On the other hand, its opposite – real-world power – may be one of the best indicators of dissent. Hence, an inquiry into powerlessness might well proceed along two different conceptual tracks.

Perhaps the reason why this attribute appears at first blush to be central to a meaningful notion of dissent is that the relatively powerless are more likely to confront the status quo as dissidents because they have more to gain and less to lose than their powerful counterparts. Yet, to the extent that their transgressions are violent, they clearly risk substantial punishment for their criminal actions. Moreover, be it violent or nonviolent, their dissent is triggered by the realistic prospect of continuing socioeconomic and political subordination due to their systemic powerlessness. We can better appreciate the alignment of dissent and powerlessness if we but consider some of those whom we typically brand as dissenters. For example, it is impossible to talk about dissent in America without mentioning the twentieth-century campaigns of at least two minority groups – the Jehovah's Witnesses' struggles for religious freedom and the African Americans' struggles for racial justice.

As the last two examples illustrate, there is often a clear relationship between the attribute of relative powerlessness and numerical minority status. After all, dissent has a "minority" aspect to it, at least insofar as the dissenter is likely to stand outside of the majoritarian mainstream. Although the dissident need not be a lone voice or a very small group, he or she must somehow be standing against the tide, and the tide most often represents the policies, practices, or conventions of the numerical majority. Most revolutionaries begin as dissenters within a numerical minority, even though a revolution may eventually become a powerful force that evolves over time into majority rule.

Still, for purposes of identifying dissent, there is no essential connection between numerical minority status and relative powerlessness. In certain regimes, such as South Africa under apartheid, a numerical minority may govern. In such a context, when the apartheid government aimed to stamp out dissent, the disempowered were a numerical majority and still relatively powerless dissenters who faced serious risks of retribution and punishment.

Recall our observation that the attribute of political powerlessness may be significant to the task of deciphering dissent, but is neither essential to nor a guarantee of dissent. This is particularly the case within scenarios of violence, as our examples of the draft-card and bank burnings evidence. If we were to accord dissenting status to both the Cantonsville Nine and the Isla Vista arsonists, it may well be because of their relative powerlessness. Then again, if we were to accord dissenting status to the former but not to the latter, an analysis of their relative powerlessness is far less determinative than an evaluation of their comparative degrees of lawlessness and violence. Because the bank burners literally turned up the flames in a far more destructive and dangerous fashion, we are disinclined to treat them as dissenters, by either a logical or linguistic measure. There is also another important difference between the two, namely the willingness of the Cantonsville Nine to accept punishment for their actions. It is to that matter that we now turn.

ACKNOWLEDGMENT OF THE RULE OF LAW AND THE ACCEPTANCE OF PUNISHMENT

Before we trouble the topic, it helps to dispense with a small conundrum. How can acceptance of the rule of law be an attribute of dissenting behavior that breaks the law? Phrased otherwise, how can one honor the law by breaching it? This hearkens back to our discussion of civil disobedience in Chapter 2. There, as here, some would not label illegal acts, especially violent ones, as dissent. But if this were to hold firm, the proud domain of dissent would diminish significantly. Only consider Roger Williams's refusal to yield to the teachings of the Church of England, Henry David Thoreau's refusal to pay a tax, or Rosa Parks's refusal to sit at the back of a bus – all of which satisfied the key characteristics of dissent but were nonetheless illegal acts in their day. To be sure, few would deny their dissenting status, for this is how most of us think and speak of such protestors. There are, therefore, strong conceptual and linguistic reasons for refusing to quarter the notion of dissent in such a manner.

That said, it might next be asked what relevance to dissent generally and to violent "dissent" in particular the attribute of acknowledgment of the rule of law and the acceptance of punishment has. Let us begin our answer by making one point clear: whatever value this attribute may have, it can do nothing to bring the likes of Leon Czolgosz (Garfield's assassin), John Wilkes Booth (Lincoln's assassin), Mark David Chapman (Lennon's assassin), Michael Frederick Griffin (Dr. Gunn's assassin), and Theodore Kaczynski ("The Unabomber") within the sanctuary of dissent. In all of these cases, the extremity of violence is beyond the redemptive work of any acceptance of responsibility, no matter how sincere.

Our observation points to the analytical work that we expect this ethical attribute to do. While this characteristic is not essential to an understanding of dissent, it can nevertheless influence us to appreciate how certain illegal or even violent acts might be viewed as dissent. Because of our usual regard for those who have the courage of their convictions and who accept responsibility and punishment for their wrongdoing, we are sometimes willing to varnish their behavior with a coat of honor. This is especially the case when we suspect that the laws or norms they are transgressing are unjust, immoral, or unconstitutional. There is also something to be said for the spirit of Socratic honor – to respect the rule of law even after one has breached a law. Much the same old-world sentiment explains our admiration for Antigone, who first challenged King Creon's burial edicts but then yielded, albeit tragically, to the larger principle of the legal order. In sum, the presence of this attribute can have an ennobling effect.

Of course, context can be everything. What may not count as dissent in a truly democratic society may be seen otherwise in a totalitarian regime. Insofar as despotic rule is the opposite of a democratic rule of law, there can be no respect for the former when gauged by the principles of the latter. The calculus of dissent alters dramatically for illegal and violent protests against brutal dictators such as Idi Amin, the tyrannical president of Uganda (1971–1979) who ordered the murder of some 300,000 of his critics. The following three commentators address this general point:

> *Cornel West:* "If you find yourself in a rule of order that has aspirations to democratic ideals, then you want to affirm those ideals even as you're willing to take the punishment for transgressive acts as a dissenter. But if, in fact, the state in which you find yourself has no moral legitimacy at all, that's different."

Noam Chomsky: "We should acknowledge and accept the rule of law when it is, to some extent at least, an expression of community will. It's a fair assumption that laws should be accepted – not in a fascist or totalitarian state, but in a moderately democratic society. Where there is at least some semblance of democracy, there is a kind of community support for the laws. Then the assumption should be that you should obey them. But it's not a binding condition."

Michael Walzer: "People engaged in acts of civil disobedience in democratic societies should be willing to accept the legal consequences of their actions. That's what makes the disobedience civil. Of course, civil disobedience is one form of dissent, but it's not the only form of dissent, for which acknowledgment of the rule of law and acceptance of punishment are less relevant."

Then, there is the question of what it means to honor the rule of law and accept punishment. When a citizen breaks the law, must he or she willingly accept legal punishment without challenge? It is one thing for a "dissenter" to evade the law; it is another to stand and contest it. In the American system of justice, citizens have a right to test the charges against them in a criminal trial and, if need be, to thereafter appeal and even challenge the constitutionality of any law. Thus, respect for the rule of law may or may not include the acceptance of punishment. Our next commentator elaborates on this:

Catharine MacKinnon: "If the purpose of dissent is to change something, part of the point is that there shouldn't be negative consequences for doing that thing. Sometimes, the purpose of dissent is to change the law. And part of resisting any consequences is to demand that there be a change in the law such that there would be no negative consequences for what you are doing."

To the extent that Professor MacKinnon means that a dissenter may use the system of law to *change* existing law, then her observation comports with the value of respecting the rule of law. And this remains so, even though her dissenter denies the legitimacy of the punishment meted out under the particular law that he or she was accused of violating.

We are now in a better position to make an informed evaluative comparison between the violent acts of the Cantonsville Nine and those of the Isla Vista radicals. As we have already noted, the difference in the magnitude of the property destruction is highly relevant. Furthermore, that the Cantonsville Nine both publicized their actions and remained on the scene to be arrested markedly differentiates them from the Bank of America arsonists who fled in the dark to elude the authorities. The coin of courage is greater than that of cowardice. Thus, we are more inclined to view the Cantonsville Nine as dissenters.

The vagaries of violence and the aforementioned attributes applicable to them reveal when and under what circumstances the concept of dissent may embrace lawlessness, even when destructive. Whether the law will legitimate such actions is another matter. Still, what a culture deems to be dissent is important and can be determinative in shaping the law's treatment of it. For in the end, if law mirrors culture, culture molds law.

CHAPTER IV

DISSENT, INC.

Dissent is not easily cabined; it resides in many quarters and goes by many names. It manifests its opposition to orthodoxy in religious realms, political circles, economic arenas, and other social and cultural contexts. How it does so – that is, how it protects and perpetuates itself – is not always as apparent as we may think. Frequently, its full face is veiled; there is sometimes more to dissent than meets the eye, more than the image of the lone dissident. By way of lifting that veil, consider the following hypothetical scenarios:

- It is 1945. Thirty Jehovah's Witnesses invade the company town of Chickasaw, Alabama. For weeks, they preach their entrenched beliefs – that Satan is the leader of the current world order; that saluting the flag, singing the national anthem, and wearing a cross are forbidden forms of idolatry; that Armageddon will cleanse the earth of sin; and that only 144,000 Christians will ascend to God's kingdom to rule with Jesus over the chastened faithful. Their evangelicalism stirs the derision and disgust of the town's folk, leading to civil unrest. Things escalate to the point that the town erects signs that read: "Private property. No trespassing. Jehovah's Witnesses strictly prohibited." Undeterred by citations and arrests for trespass, the

Witnesses continue to preach and practice their gospel.
Hoping to strike a more devastating blow, the owner of
the company town brings a civil action against the religious group for injunctive relief and compensatory and
punitive damages.

- In 1951, nine members of the House of Representatives,
  sitting as the House Un-American Activities Committee (HUAC), investigate charges of subversive threats
  and political propaganda assailing "the form of government guaranteed by our Constitution." The Committee acts pursuant to a federal law that bars Communists from working in designated government agencies
  and that bans the Communist Party USA from expend-
  ing money to promote candidates for federal office. In
  the course of the HUAC proceedings, numerous Party
  members unflinchingly reaffirm their unpopular political
  beliefs, denounce the federal law as an unconstitutional
  bill of attainder, contest the Committee's authority and
  oppressive conduct, and charge it with violating their
  constitutional rights. Nonetheless, the persecution and
  prosecution of the Communist Party continues.

- In March 1966, several hundred African-American resi-
  dents of the city and surrounding areas of Port Gibson,
  Mississippi, all of whom are members of the National
  Association for the Advancement of Colored People
  (NAACP), meet in Reverend James Dorsey's First Bap-
  tist Church. Infuriated by official inaction regarding a
  list of their particularized demands for racial equality
  and integration, they vote to engage in a collective economic boycott of local stores owned by Caucasian merchants. Over a period of three years, the NAACP stations
  "enforcers" or "deacons for defense" at the doors of the

white businesses to discourage customer patronage. The boycott succeeds beyond initial expectations and results in severe economic losses. In light of that, twenty-four retail merchants sue the NAACP for tortious interference with business and seek injunctive relief and damages in the amount of $3,542,466.

What do all of these hypothetical scenarios have in common? To be sure, they meet the core requirements of dissent, and thus qualify as dissenting activities. But unlike most of the dissidents whom we discussed earlier – such as Martin Luther, Henry David Thoreau, Eugene Debs, and Muhammad Ali – the three examples above all involve dissent by *collectivities*. That is, the dissenting activities were performed by groups, and the resentment that they generated was targeted against groups. There is something else of significance. All three groups are corporations. The Jehovah's Witnesses belong to an incorporated church; the Communists are an incorporated political party; and the interests of racial justice are the concern of NAACP, Inc.

The character of dissent is sometimes buttressed by its associational nature. It might be said that collectivities, including corporations, are surrogates for individuals; as surrogates, they defend individual rights and invigorate individual dissent. This is what we understand Professor Randy Barnett's point to be when he admonishes us to remember that the term "'corporation' is an abstraction." It is an abstraction because the corporation is "basically a form of individual association." It is "*people* who make up associations." They are the ones "who have rights and . . . may be dissenters." The fact that individuals organize in corporate form "doesn't change anything" about their status as dissenters.

Thus it is that the individual voice of dissent can be amplified by collective action. The economic power of dissent is often enhanced by collective funding and fundraising. So too, corporate status typically protects group members against individual liability. Not surprisingly, then, the NAACP has been incorporated since 1911. This fact alone suggests how vital incorporation can be to dissent.

All of this prompts us to think more about dissent in its collective form. That form may be an unincorporated association, a union, a nonprofit corporation, or even a for-profit corporation. Whereas dissent in its collective form certainly has its advantages, the question is whether it also has serious disadvantages. In other words, the issue is whether the collective form may devalue the currency of dissent to the point of bankrupting its conceptual worth. While we regularly speak of dissent in the contexts of individual conscience, individual autonomy, individual responsibility, individual decision making, and the like, it seems strained by that linguistic measure to speak of collective or corporate dissent. It is unremarkable, therefore, that some doubt whether collectivities – particularly for-profit corporations – can really be deemed dissenters. In this regard, consider the following interlocutors:

> *Faith Stevelman*: "It is a radical leap to talk about dissent of the collectivity. How much assent do we need in order to ascribe dissenting speech to an entity?"

Ralph Nader: "Executives can dissent. Individual shareholders can dissent. Employees can dissent. But not the corporate entity."

These perspectives highlight what we call the *collective intent problem* for dissent. For Stevelman and Nader, it may not ever be truly accurate to describe an entity as a dissenter unless there is unanimity among its members as to the oppositional action. With larger collectivities, whether associations, unions, or corporations, the members are so numerous and interests are so varied that it would be nearly impossible to achieve unanimous assent. Moreover, within both nonprofit and for-profit corporate forms, various constituencies – including the shareholders, managers, and employees – are not even solicited for their consent to actions taken in the corporation's name by a majority of the board of directors. What are we to make of this?

To begin thinking about the collective intent problem, it may be useful to consider what often spurs dissent – animus against a group. If Quakers dissent, it is because they are discriminated against as Quakers; if Hispanics dissent, it is because of ethnic bigotry directed against them as Hispanics; if anarchists dissent, it is because they are politically chastised as anarchists; and if gays and lesbians dissent, it is because of the animosity heaped on them as homosexuals. In all of these cases, what goads dissent is prejudice against the collectivity. By that conceptual measure, why cannot dissent respond in kind? Why, then, cannot dissent react in collective form, corporate or otherwise?

Let us not ignore the obvious. Associations do speak as associations, unions do speak as unions, churches do speak as churches, and corporations do speak as corporations. How we use our language reflects this: "The ACLU opposes police brutality." "PETA abhors animal cruelty." "The American Federation of Teachers condemns anti-union right-to-work legislation." "Google contests copyright restraints on its business practices." And when any of these groups and others speak as dissenters, we understand the groups to intend to do so. The relevant question is, by what authority does a collective entity speak for all of its members?

How a collective speaks depends on some operative rule of consensus. That rule may be one of agreement, custom, or law. In effect, the rule establishes the who and what of representational speech – in other words, who is authorized to speak for the group and in what circumstances someone is authorized to do so. In the corporate world, for example, state statutes empower a board of directors to oversee its corporation's business affairs, one of which is the issuance of public statements. If a majority of the board endorses a particular policy statement, it is an accepted legal formalism that the corporation has spoken. Furthermore, it is consistent with our language to hold that, because a majority of the board has the legal authority to speak for the corporation, the board's intentional public criticism of prevailing orthodoxy is corporate dissent.

Two examples illustrate this point. If today's political climate were similar to that of the 1890s populist movement, a state might adopt a 65 percent marginal tax rate on corporate income. Were this to happen, a corporation's board of directors would surely oppose what it views as oppressive

legislation to rob the rich. Mindful of this point, Phil Donahue has observed: "If a legislative body enacted an excessive tax on tennis shoes, Nike would be a dissenter. Wall
Street has often dissented against what it sees as the prejudice against wealth." The same would hold true, of course,
for a much smaller and less powerful corporation, such as
a family-owned manufacturing company that rails against
costly compliance with the requirements of the Americans
with Disabilities Act.

In that light, the problem of collective intent seems more
illusory than real. After all, we can distinguish between
the authorized intent of a group on the one hand and the
individual intent of its members on the other hand. The
validity of the former does not turn on the unanimity of
the latter. While there often is division within the corporate
ranks, that does not disqualify the corporation from being
an intentional dissident. Moreover, such a view comports
with how we commonly think of corporate behavior. If
Weyerhaeuser publicly denounced government restraints
on timber logging in the Sierras, or if Planned Parenthood
decried state prohibitions on third-trimester abortions, or if
the Catholic Church condemned laws requiring insurance
coverage for contraceptive services for its employees, few
would imagine that *everyone* affiliated with the corporations
shared those views.

The hollowness of the collective intent problem is aptly
depicted by the following commentator:

Anita Krug: "If Quakers, pursuant to their internal decisionmaking rules and policies, take an oppositional stance

against, for example, Maryland's abolition of its Blue Laws, and publicly push that unpopular position, then as long as the position accords with the Quakers' self-identity and purposes, a Quaker group that pickets in front of a liquor store is dissenting. To say that the group dissents does not require one to know, suspect, or even care that any particular Quaker within the group has a dissenting intention."

In dismissing one issue for collective dissent, Professor Krug flags yet another. Krug's willingness to attribute dissenting activities to the Quakers as a religious entity depends on the relationship between those activities and "the Quakers' self-identity and purposes." Restated, there must be a meaningful nexus between what is said on behalf of a group and that group's governing objectives. So long as the Quakers as a religious corporation are opposed to alcoholic consumption, then its unpopular support for a Blue Law and its liquor store picketing are bona fide group dissent. We label this the *collective legitimacy requirement* for dissent.

So long as the dissident actions of spokespersons comport with the group's identified purposes, the collective legitimacy requirement is satisfied. This requirement might be viewed as a method for discerning the presence or absence of collective intent when duly authorized members of an organization – be it a corporation, union, church, or any other association – claim to speak for the collectivity. After all, collective intent is inextricably linked to collective purpose. Corporations exist for particular reasons, and those reasons must be the lodestar by which the board navigates corporate affairs. It would be difficult to attribute a dissenting opinion to a corporation if an oppositional statement authorized by its board of directors bore no reasonable connection to the entity's raison d'etre. "Furthering what the corporation is there for," Krug adds, "helps ensure that there is 'buy-in' by the corporation's constituencies, regardless of whether they actually agree with the specific points made in any dissenting statement."

Of course, it is likely to be the case that dissent tendered in the name of a group would be understood by the public as such, even if the collective legitimacy requirement were breached. This is a revealing way of saying that perception is reality. To be sure, such a perception can be overcome if and when the breach of the collective legitimacy requirement is exposed. Imagine that the CEO of On the Road Eats, a national fast-food chain, were to make the following public statement on behalf of the corporation: "ORE supports the Ku Klux Klan's call for racial cleansing." Unquestionably, there is a disconnect between the CEO's racist stance and ORE's profit-making objectives. Predictably, there would be public blowback and loss of patronage. That might change, however, if the board of directors and shareholders issued a public statement that the CEO was not authorized to speak for ORE and expression of his personal bigotry is antithetical to the corporation's objectives.

To summarize, four points strike us as particularly germane. First, collectivities (including nonprofit and for-profit corporations) can and do dissent. Second, those who dissent in the collective name must be authorized to do so. Third, for collective dissent to exist as a formal matter, it must be congruent with collective objectives. And finally, here as elsewhere, dissent may exist as an experiential phenomenon; that is, how we perceive it and how we speak of it may trump the formal construct for dissent, unless misperceptions are corrected.

All of this invites us to consider what occurs when the collective intent problem (i.e., what is the group's actual intention?) merges with the collective legitimacy requirement (i.e., what is the group's associational purpose?). Put succinctly, can dissent endure when collective intent and purpose appear to be tied to profit making?

 CR SO

Not all corporations are created equal. We perceive, think, and talk about them differently. This is so particularly when we speak about certain for-profit corporations. Consider the way we regard a public message conveyed by *USA Today* or *CNN* as opposed to a message, even the same one, conveyed by Exxon or Pfizer. Although all are for-profit corporations, we tend to process their messages dissimilarly. This may explain why freedom of the press has been a constitutional given since 1791, whereas it took another 185-plus years before the Supreme Court extended a qualified measure of First Amendment protection to commercial speech by other for-profit corporations such as Exxon and Pfizer. What accounts for this differentiation?

However we answer this question, the *for-profit* character of a corporation cannot be the determinative factor. If it were, the public would likely perceive the messages of newspapers and pharmaceutical companies in the same way, but it does not. This illustrates what we label the *primary profit problem*: corporations like Exxon exist primarily to make money, and everything else is secondary. Translated, this problem suggests that we are disinclined to find dissent if the primary purpose behind a message is profit making. This is so even when a for-profit corporation's secondary purpose is intentional public criticism of orthodoxy. The significance of the primary profit problem is highlighted by the following commentators:

> *Geoffrey Stone*: "We normally assume that corporations are powerful, that they are the winners, and therefore there is nothing for them to dissent about. . . . If the intent of their message is basically to sell a product, then it is commercial advertising, and it's not dissent."

> *Sut Jhally*: "For-profit corporations think about making money. Their primary function is to maintain their position within the existing socioeconomic structure, and the last thing they want to do is to change or reform the world. They can present themselves as dissenters to make money, but this is only a form of branding, a symbolic transgression that is not any essential aspect of their identity."

So far as the primary profit problem is concerned, what is at stake is the issue of mixed or impure motives for dissent. This issue presents itself for individuals and collectivities alike. As to the former, recall our Chapter I hypothetical concerning pro-union picketers who, upon subsequent examination, proved to be protesting primarily for money; the "ideological commitment" of these picketers-for-hire was faithful to the highest bidder. That their primary purpose was monetary disqualified them from being authentic dissenters. The same holds true, but in a different way, with for-profit corporations.

If we posit, almost tautologically, that for-profits exist for profit, then we reasonably presume that they, like our pro-union picketers, cannot genuinely be dissenters. The cloud of monetary intention hangs heavily over any message they communicate, even if it resonates with dissenting fervor. Can this presumption be overcome? Arguably so, but in a manner conceptually distinct from that of the pro-union picketers. There, the public perception presumed the existence of dissent at the outset; that presumption was overcome only after contradictory proof of the picketers' actual subjective intent. Here, by contrast, the public presumption runs in the opposite direction; for-profit corporations are not presumed to be dissenters,* although that presumption may be overcome only after contradictory proof of the corporation's subjective intent. What could that mean? What would such corporate dissent look like?

If we do not generally associate dissent with for-profit corporations, it is because dissent is something beyond the economic raison d'etre of such corporations. The sphere of dissent is oppositional, whereas the sphere of for-profits is entrepreneurial. Oppositional intent does not typically mix well with commercial purpose. Hence, it is difficult to identify scenarios of real dissent by for-profits. That such a task is

---

* As a legal fiction, corporations are treated generally as persons for First Amendment purposes. Because the law constructs them as speakers and might by the same fiction label them as dissenters, this does not mean that we will typically perceive or speak of them as dissenters. Of course, our perceptions might change if, over time, the law were to reinforce the notion that for-profit corporations can be dissenters. If it did so in a carte blanche fashion, however, this might diminish the significance of dissent and the valuable work that it stands to do.

difficult does not mean, however, that it is altogether impossible. The next commentators ably drive this point home:

> *Kent Greenawalt*: "In theory, for-profit corporate dissent could happen, but it seems very unlikely in our culture. Could a corporation's politically oriented speech be deemed dissent? Yes, if the company really took on a dominant policy. But it's not commercially profitable to . . . be so antagonistic to dominant policy."

> *Jon O. Newman*: "For-profit corporate dissent? It's a little hard to imagine, but I suppose it's possible. A for-profit corporation could take a point of view that is very unpopular and that risks a loss of customers, in which case it would be dissenting."

> *Michael Walzer*: "If corporate intention is pure opportunism, then we would say that it might look like dissent but it isn't. Still, it's not impossible for corporate executives to have motivating ideals."

These observations pivot on the point that corporate dissent and corporate purpose are at odds; therefore, such dissent is unlikely. For dissent to exist in such circumstances, something rather aberrational must occur – Howard Zinn referred to that something as a "break-away" move. "You might have rebel activities of a limited sort," he explained. "And those particular activities might be considered acts of dissent."

Unusual as it might be, however, and difficult as it would be in light of the collective legitimacy requirement, there may be instances in which a for-profit corporation hews away from profitability and toward ideological opposition. Reconsider our example of the fast-food chain's CEO who publicly sympathized with the Ku Klux Klan's campaign of racial cleansing. If beyond that, the board of directors also endorsed this statement and the corporation suffered because of it, then we might well call that dissent.*

By contrast, what if dissent could be aligned with a profit-making purpose? After all, economic self-interest may be a strong motivator for almost any dissenter, corporate or not. Civil rights protesters are driven by their self-interest in social justice for minorities, including economic justice. Unions promote their self-interest by defending the cause

---

* Some might claim that dissent does not exist when it involves bigotry by the powerful against the powerless. Professor Catharine MacKinnon holds such a position: "Neo-Nazis and the Ku Klux Klan cannot be viewed as dissenters because they are not confronting power. They are the extreme expressions of convention. This is a society that is racist and anti-Semitic, and the Neo-Nazis and Ku Klux Klan speak for those dominant values, rather than challenging structures of power." While we find some real merit in this argument, our perspective on the matter is informed by our discussion of the attribute of relative powerlessness and its connection to dissent, offered in Chapter III. To further tease out the issue, it is formalistically conceivable that unpopular bigotry, even when embraced by a powerful individual or entity, would constitute dissent, if merely because it is an intentional public criticism of conventional norms of tolerance. The law accords with this view, as evidenced by the Supreme Court's holding in *Brandenburg v. Ohio* (1969) (sustaining the Ku Klux Klan's First Amendment right to race-hate speech). It is far more doubtful, however, that the same would hold true as a linguistic matter: Is there not something awkward about *speaking* of the Ku Klux Klan and its advocates as dissenters? Such awkwardness may well be explained for the very reasons tendered by Professor MacKinnon. All said, if the law protects such KKK "dissent," it leans more toward a formalistic understanding of dissent and away from a linguistic one. In this regard, it may be telling that the term "dissent" appears nowhere in any of the *Brandenburg* opinions. The next chapter further explores the relationship between dissent and the First Amendment.

of labor, including their own economic stability. Nonprofit organizations advance their self-interest in raising public awareness and support of their political and social objectives, including monetary support. So, is it not possible that for-profit corporations might legitimately dissent even though their economic interests are simultaneously served? Clearly, some think so:

> *Cornel West*: "Even in a corporate-dominated economy, for-profit corporations could be subject to a popular mass of vicious lies about their products. They could engage in dissent to get at the truth concerning their products' qualities."

> *Geoffrey Stone*: "Corporations may believe that the United States has minimum wage legislation that is destructive of business, or that environmental regulations are detrimental to their economic interests. In this regard, the corporations could very well dissent in the sense of trying to change both public opinion and governmental policy. On those issues, they might be relatively politically powerless and suffer societal opprobrium. . . . And even if self-interested, I would not regard this as a disqualifier for corporate dissent. There are more principled and moral and self-uninterested forms of dissent, of course, but self-interested dissent is dissent nonetheless."

Thus it is reasonable to conclude that a for-profit corporation's concern about its economic welfare should not categorically exclude it from the circle of dissenters. Mindful of what has been said in this chapter, and attentive to the foundational requirements for dissent set out in Chapter I, it may well be the case that other significant attributes of dissent discussed in Chapters II and III may help validate or invalidate a corporation's dissenting status. Primary among these would be the transgressive character of the corporation's action and a real risk of governmental sanction or social obloquy. For example, assume that Barnes & Noble launches a new series of sexual photographic e-books to tap into a burgeoning market and to test the reach of free speech law. As a result, the company is prosecuted for obscenity and is condemned by several powerful religious groups. Both as a conceptual and a linguistic matter, we might assume that, despite its mixed motives, Barnes & Noble could nonetheless qualify as a dissenter.*

To recap briefly what has been said in this section, five points merit emphasis. First, the for-profit character of a corporation cannot be a dispositive factor in determining the presence of dissent. Second, because of the primary profit problem, there is an operative presumption that for-profit corporations exist predominantly to make money, and that

---

* Of course, Barnes & Noble might also be seen as a purveyor of pornography, which raises the question of whether and under what circumstances pornography can be deemed an act of dissent challenging conventional sexual mores. Without treading too far into this thicket, suffice it to say that a pornographer might sometimes be a dissenter. Just consider a sampling from pornography's recorded history: Boccaccio's *Decameron*, the printed Italian tales of clerical seductions (1358); John Cleland's *Memoirs of a Woman of Pleasure (Fanny Hill)*, the crown jewel of the English pornographic novel (1750); the political pornography, circulated in the decades around the French Revolution, such as *Ma Constitution*, which visually portrayed General Lafayette on bended knee fondling the exposed "res publica" of Marie-Antoinette; and the 1972 opening of the controversial countercultural film, *Deep Throat*. The idea that the sexually taboo or the pictorially pornographic constitutes dissent finds expression, among other places, in Theodore Schroeder's *"Obscene" Literature and Constitutional Law: A Forensic Defense of Freedom of the Press* (New York, 1911).

purpose taints their status as dissenters. Third, that presumption might, nevertheless, be overcome if public perceptions change owing to contradictory proof of a corporation's genuine dissenting intentions. Fourth, dissent by a corporation can occur when its ideological opposition is linked to its economic self-interest. And finally, in the context of mixed motives, certain secondary attributes of dissent stand to validate the dissenting character of a corporation's actions.

CR SO

To this point, we have inquired whether collectivities can be dissenters. Before leaving this sphere, it is intriguing to inquire whether the products of for-profit corporations can color the way we view dissent. That is, can their merchandise be the canvas on which "dissent" is displayed? Put bluntly, can the messages of dissent be sold, purchased, and expressed? And when that occurs, how does that affect the way we think and talk about those messages? Such questions are particularly relevant when we consider the corporate commercial exploitation of dissent. We now turn to that topic.

Is dissent always what it appears to be? To some degree, we have considered this question already insofar as we examined the difference between the actual and perceived intentions of a "dissenter." The question deserves another look here, however, in order to explore the impact that commercialization may have on dissent.

Let us start with Ernesto Che Guevara (1928–1967), the Argentine Marxist who, together with Fidel Castro, led the

Cuban revolution. In life, Guevara was vehemently political and notoriously controversial; he was once celebrated or condemned as the enemy of capitalist power structures. In death, he became an icon; his countercultural image is ubiquitous, viewed as everything from an inspirational symbol of rebellion to an aspirational emblem of nonconformist chic. Che was once uniformly seen as the quintessential opponent of capitalism, but no more. Today, his commercialized visage serves the very capitalism he detested. To be Che-like, one need only go to Amazon.com or eBay, among many other places, to purchase a rebellious Che t-shirt, a revolutionary Che beret, a radical Che poster. In this way, it might be said that people "buy in" to dissent by branding themselves as Che.

Attentive to this, imagine a young woman who enters a Beverly Hills shopping mall wearing a red t-shirt that boldly depicts Che's portrait. She deeply sympathizes with his incendiary critique of capitalism and fervently opposes the "parasitic class" that perpetuates it. She intends to highlight the incongruity between Che's communist creed and the consumerist decadence on display throughout the mall. Although her conduct would formalistically satisfy the essential criteria for dissent, few will perceive her as a dissenter. In our modern marketplace of icons, Che's image has been commercially co-opted, and is synonymous in the public eye with the likes of James Dean, the celluloid renegade created by Hollywood.

If corporate commercialism exploits the idea of dissent or rebellion, it does so typically because Americans, in some significant way, celebrate the contrarian and romanticize the rebel. However fearful or scornful we may be of dissent in the real world, we tend to embrace or applaud dissent in the ideal world. Commercialization taps into the ideal at the expense of negating the real. That is, by commercializing dissent, corporations have sanitized it and made it safe. In doing so, however, they have also made it ineffectual and irrelevant. No one is provoked by our Che protester in the luxurious mall. Che, the revolutionary, has become Che, the fashion statement. Thus understood, there is no incongruity, there is only irony.

If the people in the shopping mall did not view the Che Guevara shirt as a symbol of protest, what did they perceive? For many who noticed the young woman clad in red and black, the garb was no more than a fashion statement, a mere aesthetic expression of the wearer's self-identity. By that measure, it made little difference if the woman had chosen instead to show off a red and black vampire t-shirt. This illustration points to what is at stake here: the distinction between dissent (however ineffective) and deviancy (however effective). That is, there is a marked difference between the instrumental use of a product to express dissent and its aesthetic use to express one's unconventionality or aberrational preferences. The former aims to criticize some orthodoxy, whereas the latter aims to make a personal statement. The former is social-centric, whereas the latter is ego-centric. The former is "insider," insofar as it focuses on reforming a group, whereas the latter is "outsider," insofar as it focuses on standing apart from the group. Wearing a black armband as an antiwar symbol is of a different order than wearing black "Demonia Disorder" Goth boots.

This is all but another way of asking the following questions: Does dissent have to be instrumental, or can it be merely self-expressive? Put differently, can dissent ever meaningfully be an aesthetic or stylistic choice of self-expression? Three of our commentators are inclined to say "no":

> *Todd Gitlin*: "My prejudice is to say [that fashion choices are generally not dissent.] This is not to say that fashion is empty, or useless, or that it could never cross the line into dissent. But I believe that it is analytically useful to preserve the category of dissent for speech or activity that aims more or less to rearrange social structures."

> *Kent Greenawalt*: "If [one's fashion choice] is just a rejection of what's going on, or it's not very well thought out, or it doesn't convey some message clearly to other people, I'm hesitant to say that it's dissent. A lot of the assertion of individuality is just an expression that one wants to be different from the norm, that conventional tastes are not going to dictate one's values. That's not enough to be dissent. To me, dissent implies disagreement, some thought-out reason that actually is the rejection of dominant elements of the culture, other than 'I just want to be my own person."

> *Fred Schauer*: "There are forms of individual self-expression that are more self-indulgent than anything else. And if we think of dissent as something that requires group membership, a dissenter really wants the rest of the group to come around. The social deviant, at least in part, doesn't care. And maybe, therefore, the term 'dissent' is not totally apt in those circumstances."

Others are a bit more equivocal, even if they tend to agree with those who distinguish between dissent and deviancy:

Howard Zinn: "I would consider [one's fashion choice] a lesser form of dissent. For me, the word 'dissent' has its greatest meaning when it is part of social action, a social struggle. Although fashion style may be a kind of personal dissent, I would like to maintain a distinction between personal expressions of dissent and expressions of dissent that form a part of a social struggle."

Geoffrey Stone: "If persons dress a certain way simply as a means of self-expression and they are not intending to convey a disagreement with the dominant culture, I would not call that dissent. But can you imagine if every law school student painted his or her hair green to protest governmental discrimination against Irish-Americans? That would clearly be both self-expression and political dissent."

Finally, there are those, like the following commentator, who more generously embrace aesthetic self-expression within the conceptual framework of dissent:

Steven Shiffrin: "I think the primary importance of dissent is instrumental, but it can be merely expressive. If [wearing Goth or hip-hop clothing] is a self-identifying activity that is contrary to existing customs, habits, traditions, and institutions, then it is dissenting. The fact that a person wears a suit the next day only indicates that he has abandoned dissent that day."

On this spectrum of opinion, we cast our lot with those who equivocate, like Zinn and Stone, by not drawing a hard-and-fast line between dissent and deviancy. We, too, maintain a distinction between the two concepts, insofar as we view dissent as more than mere deviancy, or social transgression, or aesthetic identity self-expression. Yet we recognize that there may be many examples in which it would be hard to render a categorical conclusion. After all, someone who violates a social norm or taboo can be motivated by dissent *and* other reasons, such as exhibitionism, contrarianism, juvenility, or individuality. Here, again, we see the issue of mixed intentions.

One final consideration affects our calculus: the importance of preserving, as best as one reasonably can, the valence of dissent. That is, the more the notion of dissent is diluted, the less substantial its value. If one is profligate in equating dissent with deviancy, the unfortunate result is the trivialization and diminution of the concept. As a consequence, it is easy to conflate the purely personal with the significantly social. The late American historian and social activist, Howard Zinn, minced no words in this regard: "Too often, individual expressions of cultural dissent may substitute for more important actions, and may delude persons into thinking that they are doing something significant when they are not. Surely, they are doing something important insofar as they are expressing themselves, but that can be a diversion that takes energy away from something larger." We concur.

Throughout this chapter, we have focused on the meaning of dissent within two special contexts: the expressive activities of collectivities, particularly for-profit corporations, and the expressive activities of consumers who use commercial products for purposes that may or may not be understood as dissent. In various ways, our analysis of these contexts has demonstrated the attributes of dissent at work and has underlined their essentiality in how we both define and speak of dissent.

CHAPTER V

DISSENT AND LAW'S PARAMETERS

Without dissent the First Amendment would be meaningless. If the Constitution protected no more than speech with which we agreed, there would be nothing in need of protection. The unorthodox, the nonconformist, the outcast and their like give vital life to the First Amendment. Without protecting them, the First Amendment would be little more than a parchment admonition – a gospel to be preached on Sunday and flouted every other day.

Think of the work that the First Amendment does. It safeguards the speech of those who refute our creeds, reject our values, renounce our government, and even repudiate our very way of life. This uniquely American principle of free speech provides a haven for irritating ranters and irksome rogues who feel the need to spoil our parade. In short, it protects the voice of the other. And whose voice is that? It is the voice of the dissenter.

There is something romantic about the idea of dissent, which helps explain why we cherish it. Ideally, we as a people want to be open-minded; we want to be tolerant when it comes to any variety of opposing religious, political, or cultural views. We admire the daring man who stands up when others sit down; we admire those who have the courage of their convictions. The iconic value of dissent cannot be overemphasized. Offensive as it was to some at the time, who can forget that morning in October 1968 when two African Americans (gold medalist Tommie Smith and bronze medalist John Carlos) raised their fists in brazen protest when they stood on the podium to receive their Olympic medals? Or recall Mary Beth Tinker and the black armband she wore to her high school class to protest the Vietnam War. So great is the iconic significance of that act of dissent that her armband is today enshrined in a glass case at the Newseum in Washington, DC, for all to see and admire.

We endure dissent precisely because we value freedom. Justice Louis Brandeis heroically championed that principle in his famous concurrence in *Whitney v. California* (1927). In words that could be etched in stone, he wrote: "Those who won our independence by revolution were not cowards. They did not fear political change. They did not exalt order at the cost of liberty." These "self-reliant" Americans had an abiding "confidence in the power of free and fearless reasoning." That confidence is what animates our faith in freedom and our toleration of dissent. This, at least, is the aspirational ideal, which is honored in our finest moments.

It was not one of those moments when the spirit of dissent was suppressed not long after the First Amendment became the law of the land. Only consider the story of Benjamin Bache (1769–1798). This Philadelphia printer was the publisher of the *Aurora*, the anti-Federalist paper dedicated to attacking George Washington and Alexander

Hamilton and virtually everything they did in the name of foreign policy. Bache was acerbic, caustic, vile, vituperative, uncontrollable, scurrilous, and often mean-spirited. He was relentless and severe in his criticisms of the Federalists. John Fenno, the editor of the *Gazette of the United States*, a Federalist-sympathetic paper, lashed out in kind: "Mr. Bache . . . seems to take a kind of hellish pleasure in defaming the name of WASHINGTON."

Nothing fazed Bache. When President Washington stepped down (some say because of Bache), the editor of the *Aurora* then directed his spite toward John Adams. "Old, querulous, bald, blind, crippled, toothless Adams" is how he described the president he loved to loathe. Abigail Adams despised her husband's tormenter; in her eyes, he was vile and treacherous. She once confided to her sister, Mary Cranch: "Scarcely a day passes but some such scurrility appears in Bache's paper, very often unnoticed, and of no consequence in the minds of many people, but it has, like vice of every kind, a tendency to corrupt the morals of common people. Lawless principles," she emphasized, "naturally produce lawless actions."

Largely in response to Benjamin Bache and his anti-Federalist cohorts, on July 14, 1798, John Adams signed the infamous Alien and Sedition Acts. The latter made it criminal to "write, print, utter, or publish" any "false, scandalous and malicious writing or writings against the government of the United States, or either House of the Congress of the United States, or of the President of the United States" with "intent to defame" any such parties or to bring them "into contempt or disrepute; or to excite against them . . . the

hatred of the good people of the United States, or to stir up
sedition within the United States; or to excite any unlawful
combinations therein, for opposing or resisting any law of
the United States." The sanctions: "a fine not exceeding two
thousand dollars, and . . . imprisonment not exceeding two
years." With this Act, as Professor Geoffrey Stone observed,
"the Federalists (and the U.S. government) declared war on
dissent."

Unwilling to wait for Adams's signature on the bill, Federalist prosecutors hauled Bache off to court on June 26,
1798, and charged him with violating the federal common
law of seditious libel, this for "libeling the President & the
Executive Government, in a manner tending to excite sedition, and opposition to the laws, by sundry publications and
re-publications."

At last, the "seditious printer" had been arrested; now his
"scurrilous rants" would cease. But things did not play out
that way – the day after his arrest, Bache vowed in the *Aurora*
never to abandon "the cause of truth and republicanism,"
which he pledged to honor to "the best of his abilities, while
life remains."

But it was all for naught, for late on the evening of
Monday, September 10, 1798, Benjamin Bache died, thus
ending his prosecution before his trial began. With Bache
dead, the *Aurora*'s presses were temporarily stilled. Mean-
while, given the Adams administration's new sedition law
to silence its political enemies, the Anti-Federalists had
good cause to fear their fate. In a letter of October 11,
1798, Vice-President Thomas Jefferson warned Senator

Stevens Thompson Mason that the Sedition Act was "merely an experiment on the American mind to see how far it will bear an avowed violation of the Constitution." During the course of that experiment, Anti-Federalist dissenters were persecuted and prosecuted for another two years.

Relief finally came to the Anti-Federalists. Jefferson prevailed in the presidential election of 1800, and pardoned those convicted under the Alien and Sedition Acts. Those laws expired on March 3, 1801. With that, the spirit of the First Amendment returned like a great phoenix. Dissent was once again legal.

Today, the Alien and Sedition Acts are viewed as quintessential violations of our First Amendment freedoms.* They are synonymous with tyranny; to invoke them is to condemn them. While the Supreme Court never had to pass on the legitimacy of these laws, their unconstitutionality is unquestioned. As Justice William Brennan aptly put it: "Although the Sedition Act was never tested in this Court, the attack upon its validity has carried the day in the court of history."

∞ ∞

The Benjamin Baches of our day are the beneficiaries of First Amendment safeguards that stand to protect their seething political harangues. We do not question that such

---

* The same, of course, could be said of the Espionage Act of 1917 and the Sedition Act of 1918.

tirades, particularly when delivered in print, fall squarely within the fundamental freedoms of speech and press. Given that, it is important to recognize that the relationship between dissent and the First Amendment is more opaque than one might first perceive. That is so because the concepts are not co-extensive. Looking at the relationship from a First Amendment standpoint, it is clear that there is a considerable amount of expression covered under the First Amendment that would be difficult or impossible to characterize as dissent. Much oral, print, and digital expression relating to literature, music, painting, film, scientific writing, and commercial advertising does not constitute dissent, if only because it is not intended to criticize any orthodoxy or established law, policy, or practice.

Looking at the relationship from the standpoint of dissent, however, we are invited to ask: To what extent is dissent to be privileged under the First Amendment's protection? Let us begin this analysis with a bold declaration by a Supreme Court Justice. In the throes of one of the most contentious times in U.S. history, Justice William O. Douglas released his *Points of Rebellion* (1969). The dust jacket described the book as "a somber warning to all Americans" that foretold of an "impending and inevitable revolution in the nation . . . unless the Establishment responds to the urgency of current protest with fundamental and wide-ranging social reform." On the first page of the text, Douglas starkly stated: "All dissenters are protected by the First Amendment." What did that mean? Could such absolutist words be taken literally? Did Douglas intend to confine his statement only to dissenting activities that were unquestionably legal, such as civil protest? Or did he purport to include illegal activities as well, such as civil disobedience? In this regard, our commentators' responses vary:

> *Jon O. Newman:* "You would have to ask how Justice Douglas defines dissent. He may hold this view because he's defined dissent narrowly."

> *Martha Nussbaum:* "We don't know whether the statement is true or ludicrously false. Does Douglas include as dissent a libelous remark made with reckless disregard of the truth? Does he include as dissent unlicensed medical advice that intends to contradict established medical knowledge and practice, and so on? Certainly those cases are not protected by the First Amendment. And there's a lot of speech apart from that – fighting words or obscenity, for example – that somebody might defend as dissent and that is not protected by the First Amendment as currently interpreted."

> *Kent Greenawalt:* "If we understand dissent as covering illegal activities, I think it's obviously wrong.... I don't think everything we would call dissent should be protected by the First Amendment."

> *Steven Green:* "Is Douglas's statement aspirational? Yes, because the First Amendment protects an ideological perspective, but it doesn't protect it within certain illegal actions associated with that. What I see Douglas as saying is that all ideas and objections to the powers that be are fully protected by the First Amendment when they are verbally expressed. But there are certainly going to be practical limitations placed upon dissent outside those boundaries."

One key takeaway point is that the concept of dissent is not necessarily synonymous with the First Amendment protection of dissent. As Albert Camus put it: "There are means that cannot be excused." In other words, there must be parameters. How dissent is defined will determine whether or not it is constitutionally permissible.

By that measure, if the concept of dissent is narrowly defined, all dissent would be constitutional. If the notion of dissent were to mean no more than civil protests that comply with the restrictions of common law and statutory law, then dissent would have no need for the First Amendment. But such simplicity belies the complexity of what is at stake here. Over the span of U.S. history, majoritarian mandates were quite often insensitive to minoritarian rights of peaceful dissent. A few illustrations buttress this point:

- *Abolition of Slavery*: With the publication of abolitionist tracts during the antebellum period, Southerners blamed Northern antislavery propaganda for inciting unrest among their slaves. In 1830, Mississippi enacted a law forbidding the circulation of "seditious pamphlets," such as abolitionist works; punishment for violations included jailing for any white and execution for any black. Alabama was particularly harsh, demanding the death penalty for publication and distribution of "any seditious papers...tending to produce conspiracy or insurrection...among the slaves or colored population." Within a few years, every Southern state had adopted laws prohibiting abolitionist expression in one way or another.
- *Labor Picketing*: In the early 1900s, the Industrial Workers of the World ("Wobblies") often engaged in peaceful free speech tactics (hyperbolically called "free speech fights") to spread their messages of "the emancipation of

the working-class from the slave bondage of capitalism."
A single Wobbly would proclaim his revolutionary screed
on a street corner; once he was arrested for vagrancy or
breach of the peace and hauled away, another Wobbly
would begin speaking similarly on the same spot, and so
on. During the 1909 "free speech fights" in Spokane,
Washington, police arrested some 1,200 Wobblies, jam-
ming 28 of them at a time into a 7-by-8-foot jail cell.
When the authorities asked to see their protest permits,
Wobblies would respond that they "had none save the
First Amendment."

- *Women's Suffrage*: In 1917, it was unlawful for suffragettes
  in the National Women's Party to protest as "Sentinels
  of Liberty" in front of the White House – nearly 500
  women were arrested and many jailed.
- *The Red Scare*: Inspired by the anticommunist crusade of
  Attorney General A. Mitchell Palmer, many states passed
  criminal anarchy or criminal syndicalism statutes forbidding antigovernment advocacy, and thirty-two states
  enacted criminal laws forbidding the display of the red
  flag in symbolic protest. "In 1919–1920, at least 1,400
  individuals were arrested under such legislation, and
  at least 300 were convicted and sentenced to terms of
  imprisonment ranging up to twenty years."

These and other laws reflect a mindset that conditions
free speech rights on the beneficence of lawmakers. The
length and breadth of a right is determined less by constitutional declarations than by legislative decrees. Theodore
Schroeder, a noted nineteenth-century free speech advocate, took strong exception to this, labeling it "liberty
by permission." Harking back to the British censorship

tradition of print licensing, Schroeder decried a state "in which we will enjoy any liberties only by permission, not as a matter of right."

Importantly, it is largely because of the varnish of the modern First Amendment that today we would acknowledge that the sphere of civil protests and other legitimate forms of dissent cannot be cabined by ordinary law. Hence, Professor Nadine Strossen admonishes us to remember: "The mere fact that you are transgressing a law should not be enough to take you out of the legitimate realm of dissent because the law could be unconstitutional." Thus, the work to be done by the First Amendment is precisely that of expanding the parameters of dissent beyond the narrow strictures of common law and statutes. To that point we now turn.

സ ഇ

Imagine someone claiming a "right" to:

- impugn another's reputation
- invade another's privacy
- inflict emotional distress
- violate school rules
- interfere with the profitability of a commercial business
- trespass on private property
- ignore an antinoise ordinance
- express vulgarities in a courthouse
- loiter
- engage in disorderly conduct
- breach the peace
- advocate illegal action.

Standing alone, how likely is it that anyone would seriously argue for these "rights"? Claims to contravene the civil and criminal laws regulating such behavior would strike most of us as preposterous. If the law is to yield in any of these situations, something more must be added to the conceptual mix. That something might well be the First Amendment aligned with particular kinds of dissent.

It is a phenomenon easily underappreciated: the First Amendment serves a monitoring function in curbing the excesses of civil and criminal law in the interests of dissent. That is, there is a functional relationship between the First Amendment and dissent, insofar as the former pushes back civil and criminal sanctions in order to provide sufficient breathing room for dissent.

This functional relationship hinges on two basic points: (1) the First Amendment works to legitimize certain kinds of speech or action that were previously contrary to law; and (2) this result may be more likely when the expression can be fairly categorized as dissent, although of a certain kind. It is in this way, then, that questions of law and language merge. That is, before an issue becomes a constitutional one, it is first a philosophical one, and how we think about and speak of dissent very much influences the ways lawmakers, policy makers, executive officials, and courts respond to expression that might not otherwise be tolerated. Let us now tease out these points a bit more.

It is textbook law: "political speech . . . is central to the meaning and purpose of the First Amendment." For many, as Justice Clarence Thomas has noted, "political speech is the primary object of First Amendment protection." In that constitutional calculus, the Supreme Court has been emphatic: the "First Amendment requires us to err on the side of protecting political speech rather than suppressing it." For such reasons and others, "it would be dangerous," to say the least, for government to "regulate core political speech." But what makes political speech so special? Why do we value it so dearly as to place it on the highest rung of protected expression?

Over time, many jurists and scholars have given various answers to these questions. But one merits our special attention here, and it is this: dissent is central to any idea of political speech. It cannot be taken out of the beaker of political expression without altering the basic chemistry. Dissent gives vitality to political speech. To reiterate, if political speech meant no more than expressing ideas acceptable to the polis, there would be no need to shield it. We protect political speech precisely because we cherish dissent, because we respect the rights of others to air political views different from our own. It is dissent that makes a robust exchange of views in the marketplace of ideas possible. Moreover, if the First Amendment aims to check the powers of government, realizing that objective is only possible if the constitutional guarantee fosters divergent views.

Something of the same also might be said of religious speech protected under the Free Exercise Clause of the First Amendment. As the history of humankind reveals, dissent is key to any meaningful notion of religious freedom. The very ethos for breaking away from the rule of the papacy or that of the Church of England was to permit, and even encourage, the kind of religious freedom that did not otherwise comport with the official religion of the state.

If political speech is at the core of the First Amendment, and dissent is at the core of political speech, we come to value the former by appreciating the parameters of the latter. By the same token, if religious speech is vital to religious freedom safeguarded by the First Amendment, and dissent is at the core of religious speech, we come to value the former by appreciating the parameters of the latter. All of this is another way of saying that the work of the First Amendment is, in important measure, inextricably linked to dissent and how we comprehend it.

In one way or another, the idea of dissent finds followers in every ideological camp, even if they may not always express their dissent within that camp itself. Dissent has a certain idealistic cache, particularly when political or religious dissent is involved, and that largely explains why we value it. In that vein, Benjamin Franklin observed that "[i]t is the first responsibility of every citizen to question authority." Moreover, as President Lincoln suggested, there is something noble about dissent: "If there is anything that links the human to the divine, it is the courage to stand by a principle when everybody else rejects it." To much the same effect, Dr. Martin Luther King admonished Americans: "One has a moral responsibility to disobey unjust laws." Or as Christopher Hitchins, ever the contrarian, put it by way of a more critical perspective: "If you want to stay in for the long haul, and lead a life that is free from illusions either propagated by you or embraced by you, then I suggest you learn to recognize and avoid the symptoms of the zealot and the person who knows he is right. For the dissenter, the skeptical mentality is at least as important as any armor of principle." Though perhaps not explicitly, when a First Amendment claim to dissent is sustained, the unstated reason may have much to do with the venerable ethos associated with dissent.

It is almost axiomatic: if properly understood, the notion of dissent stands to expand the domain of the First Amendment, properly interpreted. In the process, the First Amendment sometimes converts illegal action into lawful action; it transforms what was seen as anarchy into what may be viewed as democratic engagement; and it reconfigures the relationship between society and its critics. Again, this is the work that philosophy does (how we define or speak of dissent) when acting in tandem with the First Amendment (how legislatures and courts go about protecting dissent). A few more examples should help clarify our thinking.

First Amendment Expansion in the Service of Student Dissent: It was a period of escalating tension. America's war against North Vietnam's communists had already taken the lives of almost 2,000 soldiers, and the nation's youth – disgruntled with their government's military designs and anxious over their own personal destinies – had begun to voice their opposition. Thirteen-year-old Mary Beth Tinker, the child of a Methodist minister, was among those caught up in the antiwar sentiment. Late in December 1965, she planned, along with a few of her public high school friends, to express "grief over the deaths of soldiers and civilians in Vietnam" by wearing black armbands in class. Hearing of the prospective student protest, the principals in the school district of Des Moines, Iowa, speedily issued a new policy; it prohibited armband protests and authorized the suspension of any violator. "The schools are no place for demonstrations," declared Raymond Peterson, the district's director of secondary education. "The educational program would be disturbed by students wearing arm-bands." On Thursday, December 16, Mary Beth wore her black arm-band. Although a few boys made "smart remarks" during lunch, she recalled, morning classes progressed without incident. By the afternoon, however, she had been suspended.

Unquestionably, at this time the state of the law favored the school district's censorial actions. The Supreme Court had never decisively enunciated the First Amendment rights of students within a public school setting, and prior lower court decisions had ruled that the best interests of the schools were served by the maintenance of an orderly and disciplined student body. So, it was not surprising that when Leonard Tinker, Mary Beth's father, brought a civil rights action against the school district, the federal trial court dismissed the case. According great deference to the discretion of the school district authorities, the judge reasoned: "Unless the actions of school officials . . . are unreasonable, the Courts should not interfere."

When the matter of *Tinker v. Des Moines Independent Community School District* (1969) came before the Supreme Court, Justice Hugo Black – the great champion of free speech – thought this a straightforward case. As he put it during discussion with his brethren in private conference, there "is no First Amendment problem." And as he later reaffirmed in his *Tinker* opinion, if sustained, the relief sought by the petitioner would usher in "an entirely new era" in the constitutional law of school governance. That was as good as any general statement of existing First Amendment law prior to *Tinker*. As fate had it, however, Black's was a dissenting view.

By a 7–2 majority, the high court sustained Tinker's First Amendment claim. With rhetorical flourish, Justice Abe Fortas's opinion for the Court proclaimed: "It can hardly be argued that either students or teachers shed their constitutional rights to freedom of speech or expression at the schoolhouse gate." Recognizing that such fundamental rights might "collide with the rules of the school authorities," Fortas articulated a balancing standard: student speech rights are to be protected unless school officials can prove that the expression would "materially and substantially interfere with the requirements of appropriate discipline in the operation of the school" or otherwise encroach on the rights of others.

Symbolically speaking, Mary Beth Tinker's black armband was the "voice" of the other. It was an example of the dissident spirit of American revolutionary history being brought into the classroom. Quiet and peaceful, serious and poignant, her political message bore all the earmarks of honorable dissent. Because of that, it garnered the sympathies of a majority of the justices who were otherwise disinclined to trammel the authority of public school officials. Then, as now, it took something more than novel legal arguments to give the First Amendment a foothold in the classroom. In important part, that something more was dissent. If the Court has refused to extend the *Tinker* principle, it is largely because the character of dissent displayed by Mary Beth Tinker has been notably absent.

First Amendment Expansion in the Service of Dissenting Defamation: When Montgomery, Alabama, Police Commissioner Lester Sullivan sued the *New York Times* for defamation in 1960, a few matters of law were well established: (1) First and Fourteenth Amendment freedoms constrained only state action, and not private action; (2) libel was excluded from free speech protections under the First and Fourteenth Amendments; (3) Alabama common law deemed a publication to be libelous per se if the published statements tended to injure a person in his reputation or profession or to subject the person to public contempt.

The controversy in *New York Times v. Sullivan* centered on a contentious full-page political advertisement, entitled "Heed Their Rising Voices," that had been purchased by a civil rights group. "As the whole world knows by now," the ad began, "thousands of Southern Negro students are engaged in widespread non-violent demonstrations in positive affirmation of the right to live in human dignity as guaranteed by the U.S. Constitution and the Bill of Rights.... [T]hey are being met by an unprecedented wave of terror by those who would deny and negate that document.... Again and again the Southern violators have answered Dr. King's peaceful protests with intimidation and violence." In the same forceful tone, the ad continued: "Small wonder that the Southern violators of the Constitution fear this new, non-violent brand of freedom fighter ... even as they fear the upwelling right-to-vote movement. Small wonder that they are determined to destroy the one man who, more than any other, symbolizes the new spirit now sweeping the South – the Rev. Dr. Martin Luther King, Jr., world-famous leader of the Montgomery Bus Protest." As it turned out, there were some small factual errors in the advertisement, which raised big defamation problems.

In a landmark ruling that changed the constitutional law of defamation, the Supreme Court revised the established legal doctrines: (1) First and Fourteenth Amendment freedoms can constrain private actors in the defamation area; (2) certain forms of libel are entitled to constitutional protection; (3) the common law of libel in the nation, including that of Alabama, must be revised to accommodate expression critical of governmental officials. The syndicated columnist Anthony Lewis labeled the *Sullivan* opinion a "revolutionary decision" for libel law. The revered First Amendment scholar Alexander Meiklejohn viewed the impressive breadth of the decision as "an occasion for dancing in the streets." And the respected constitutionalist Alexander M. Bickel recognized the Court's rationales as virtually "declaring the Sedition Act of 1798 unconstitutional, more than a century and a half after its expiration." Considering *Sullivan* along with other free speech cases of the era, Bickel opined: "The First Amendment decisions of the Supreme Court, in part, incorporate a 'right to disobey,' a right that has been controlled and stylized. The amendment makes allowance for domesticated civil disobedience much after the fashion of exemptions for conscientious objection."

It is a fact all too commonly ignored: but for the posture of the case – combining protest and racial equality – Justice William Brennan's seminal ruling in *New York Times v. Sullivan* (1964) might never have occurred. Before this time, 183 years of established law pointed in the opposite direction and placed serious impediments on sociopolitical dissenters and those who disseminated their messages. The law of defamation could break the backs of social movements and their publishers. To avoid such obstacles, "Justice Brennan wisely redrew traditional lines of constitutional understanding in the face of a massive demand by people of color for the equality they had long been denied. This is what makes *Sullivan* above all else a civil rights case."

First Amendment Expansion in the Service of Dissenting Advocacy of Illegal Action: The Ohio Criminal Syndicalism Act, passed in 1919 during the period of the Red Scare, made it illegal to "advocate . . . the duty, necessity, or propriety of crime, sabotage, violence, or unlawful methods of terrorism" for political reform, or to assemble with any group "to teach or advocate" such activity. Twenty states had adopted identical or similar laws from 1917 to 1920.

Clarence Brandenburg, the leader of the Ohio Ku Klux Klan, organized a Klan rally at a farm in Hamilton County. Addressing a handful of hooded members gathered around a burning wooden cross, Brandenburg warned: "We're not a revengent (sic) organization, but if our President, our Congress, our Supreme Court, continues to suppress the white, Caucasian race, it's possible that there might have to be some revengeance (sic) taken." On the basis of these remarks, he was arrested and convicted under the syndicalism act, fined $1,000, and sentenced to imprisonment for one to ten years.

For almost twenty years prior to *Brandenburg v. Ohio* (1969), Supreme Court precedents, with few exceptions, had strengthened state police powers to criminalize mere advocacy of violence. But, in a unanimous *per curiam* opinion (authored by Justice William Brennan), the Court reworked its First Amendment doctrine to protect Brandenburg's unsavory rant. "[T]he constitutional guarantees of free speech and free press do not permit a State to forbid or proscribe advocacy of the use of force or of law violation," the Court wrote, "except where such advocacy is directed to inciting or producing imminent lawless action and is likely to incite or produce such action."

Given *Brandenburg*'s stringent standard, today's criminal statutes can only reach obviously intentional, highly probable, and immediate incitements to illegal activity. Clearly, the decision effectively undermined the regime of criminal syndicalism. Additionally, it buttressed First Amendment rights in other criminal contexts, such as the protection afforded to flag desecration in the controversial flag-burning case of *Texas v. Johnson* (1989); and it paved the way for the extension of free speech safeguards into the realm of civil liability for incitement, as evidenced in the constitutional protection accorded to economic boycotts in *NAACP v. Claiborne Hardware Company* (1982). In this light, Professor Steven Shiffrin forcefully makes a telling point: "The cases involving the advocacy of illegal action are strong examples of effecting change in criminal law out of respect for the values of dissent."

In one regard, the line between *New York Times v. Sullivan* and *Brandenburg v. Ohio* is a long one; in another regard, it is a short one. On the one hand, *Sullivan* and

Brandenburg are antithetical: the former recruited the First
Amendment in the service of racial justice, and the latter
invoked it in the name of racial bigotry. On the other hand,
the two cases have something fundamental in common: both
are bulwarks of dissent. It is a sign of the high value given to
the conceptual currency of dissent that the same liberal Justice William Brennan authored both opinions to safeguard
the full spectrum of dissent – to protect not only expression
that we revere, but also that which we revile. To borrow a line
from Oliver Wendell Holmes, Jr., "if there is any principle
of the Constitution that more imperatively calls for attachment than any other, it is the principle of free thought – not
free thought for those who agree with us, but freedom of
thought that we hate."

If, as in earlier chapters, we have been unwilling to champion the idea of dissent in extreme forms (i.e., terrorism or
assassination), it is in part because we are sensitive to the
work that the First Amendment stands to do in vindicating
the right to express divergent views. That work – moving
certain types of expression from lawlessness to lawfulness –
cannot occur if there is no restraining principle, no way
to rein in definitional and rhetorical excesses. By the same
token, that First Amendment work may be long in coming,
if ever, before it covers particular forms of expression or
action that fall under the conceptual or linguistic umbrella
of dissent (i.e., civil disobedience). Liberty operates on a
historical continuum, and in that process, what was yesterday's crime may be tomorrow's right. On this point, we
respectfully defer to one of our commentators:

Nadine Strossen: "There are activities that now are still considered to be legitimately criminalized, but a future generation may look back on our time and say that the crime was actually the exercise of dissent that should have been recognized as a First Amendment right."

Dissent, duly defined, is like a seed stirring in the soil, waiting to blossom in the sunlight of the future. In that respect, the law of the First Amendment is rooted in the ground of philosophy – theory precedes precedent.

CR SO

The enterprise of moving dissent across the line from lawlessness to lawfulness is not entirely within the province of First Amendment jurisprudence. It is also within the domain of other strands of constitutional and ordinary law, both as proclaimed and practiced. Some attention, then, must be given to that domain in order to more fully appreciate the relationship between dissent and law's parameters.

Beyond the First Amendment and its state counterparts, two other legal doctrines have occasionally succeeded in legitimizing dissent that originally was the focus of criminal or civil constraints. The first of these is the void-for-vagueness doctrine, which appeals to the requirements of adequate "notice" embedded in the due process guarantees of the Fifth and Fourteenth Amendments.* Generally stated, the doctrine holds that a statute or regulation may be

---

* So far as free expression cases are concerned, the void-for-vagueness defense is often raised in tandem with a First Amendment substantial overbreadth defense. Under the latter, a statute or regulation is deemed unconstitutionally overbroad if it proscribes substantially more expression than necessary in order to achieve the government's otherwise legitimate purposes.

invalidated if a reasonable person could not tell from the terms of the law what is prohibited and what is permitted. Over time, the Supreme Court has adjusted the plate tectonics of legitimate dissent by striking down unconstitutionally vague restrictions on various types of civil protest, such as nonviolent political demonstrations, non-obstructionist labor picketing, and the mere advocacy of subversion to overturn the constituted system of government.

The second doctrine is the necessity defense sometimes raised in criminal law prosecutions. Distinguished from the private necessity privilege in tort law or the right of self-defense for the use of force in times of danger, the necessity defense – particularly when it is raised in civil disobedience trials – provides an opportunity for a judge or jury "to expand the evaluation of otherwise criminal conduct beyond the letter of particular prohibitions." Law Professor William P. Quigley, a civil liberties litigator and scholar, appreciates the attractiveness of the necessity defense to civil disobedients. "[I]t allows them to deny guilt without renouncing their socially driven acts," he explains. "It offers a means to discuss political issues in the courtroom, a forum in which reformers can demand equal time and, perhaps, respect."

Furthermore, by pleading and proving the elements of the necessity defense, civil disobedients are empowered to debate, justify, and publicize their political motivations:

- "In proving the imminence of the harm, they can demonstrate the urgency of the social problem."
- "In showing the relative severity of the harms, they can show the seriousness of the social evil they seek to avert."

- "In establishing the lack of reasonable alternatives, they can assault the unresponsiveness of those in power in dealing with the problem and prod them to action."
- "And in presenting evidence of a causal relationship, they can argue the importance of individual action in reforming society."

Had the necessity defense been recognized in antiquity, the fate of Antigone and Socrates may well have been different. In more modern times, judicial tolerance of the necessity defense doctrine has waxed and waned, with federal courts being more skeptical of it than their state counterparts; their concern is that liberal application of the doctrine would undermine the rule of law by promoting jury nullification. Nonetheless, what is important about the defense, in its pristine form, is the accommodation that law makes in the name of dissent. Just as the Supreme Court gave elasticity to the First Amendment in the civil rights era, so may future courts come to appreciate the value of embracing more generously the necessity defense.

Although crimes of dissent may not be explicitly sheltered by constitutional and ordinary law doctrines, operational practices of governmental officials may effectively save dissidents from harsh sanctions. Within the realm of executive powers, the police may believe the age-old adage that discretion is the better part of valor, and may choose not to strictly enforce the letter of the law against civil and uncivil protestors. Similarly, prosecutors may avert their eyes from enforcement of criminal mandates against violators reasonably motivated by the spirit of nonviolent dissent. And, of course, presidential or gubernatorial pardons can be granted to the convicted dissenters whose causes resonate with public sentiments. Along the enforcement chain, the judiciary may also play a significant role as the guardians of dissent; judges can so act in their capacities as triers of fact or determiners of sentences. One of our judicial commentators weighs in on several of these operational practices:

> *Jon O. Newman*: "The first question is whether we should have a law that impacts nonviolent dissenting activity at all. Once we have a law, should a prosecutor bring the case? That's a second question. Once a prosecutor brings the case, should the judge find him guilty? That's a third question. And then near the end of the chain, there are still other questions. Should the sentence be very lenient, because of the social value of the protest and the minimal inconvenience to the public weal? Or should it be harsh in the cases where the public is seriously inconvenienced?"

∞ ∞

Isegoria. It is the ancient Greek word for equality in freedom of speech. In a sense, it is a strange idea – the notion of giving an equal say to the speech of the other, even one's opponent. The basic message is not that all ideas are equal, but that all ideas ought to have an equal chance in competing for the minds of men and women.

But minds can be fickle; more than mere ideas may be necessary. Provocation is sometimes more important than illumination. If dissenters are prickly, it is because they prick us in ways that upset the equilibrium of the status quo, that disturb the balance of our political compromises, and that shake the very foundations of our belief systems. Little wonder, then, that over the ages the dissenter has been branded a heretic, a traitor, an instigator, or a rebel – all who yearn to build tomorrow's utopias on the rubble of today's dystopias.

Strange, then, that the law should protect the dissenter from the understandable intolerance of the *demos*. The lesson of two thousand-plus years, however, is the lesson of the First Amendment. It is a lesson in limits – that the parameters of ordinary law must sometimes yield to the principle of the First Amendment in the name of dissent.

EPILOGUE

The noble title of "dissident" must be earned rather than claimed; it connotes sacrifice and risk rather than mere disagreement, and it has been consecrated by many exemplary and courageous men and women.

– Christopher Hitchins

In the annals of Anglo-American dissent, few have earned as much respect and ridicule as Thomas Paine. Born in 1737, he was a patriot to the colonies and a traitor to the Crown. He valued constitutional government, yet had a radical bent. He believed in God, but detested organized religion. He was allied with the great men and ideas of his day, yet often kept a skeptical distance from both. Others were willing to declare their grievances, but this British citizen demanded nothing short of independence from the motherland.

Paine's *Common Sense*, published in the winter of 1776, has been hailed as "the single most influential political work in American history." An astonishing 150,000 copies of the 2-shilling pamphlet, carrying rousing messages about rights and revolution coupled with broadsides against monarchical rule, were snatched up in its first few months. *Common Sense* took its message to the common folk; no less a figure than General George Washington thought the work had produced "a powerful change . . . in the minds of many men." Paine wrote with "a rage and a fury that none of the founding fathers ever expressed. He spoke out of a deep anger shared by . . . artisans, shopkeepers, traders, and petty merchants." Little wonder, then, that his tract "did not merely change minds, it inflamed passions." The rest is history, both glorious and ruinous.

At Paine's funeral on June 9, 1809, no statesmen or dignitaries paid their respects to this darling of the American Revolution. "No eulogies were offered when Paine's coffin was lowered into the ground." His glory waned and his ruin waxed, in important part because of the 1793 publication of *The Age of Reason*, his provocative assault on established religion. "I do not believe," he wrote, "in the creed professed by . . . any church I know of. My own mind is my own church." This Deist son of an Anglican mother and a Quaker father had once preached as a Methodist, but now published words that outraged many of those who formerly adored him. Samuel Adams lambasted Paine's efforts to "unchristianize the mass of our citizens." For John Adams, Paine was a "satyr" begotten by a "wild boar on a bitch wolf" who led "a career of mischief." Many decades later, Paine was still misunderstood as godless; then-Governor Theodore Roosevelt denounced him as a "filthy little atheist."

With time, America's views of this great dissident came full circle. Theodore Roosevelt's distant cousin, President Franklin Delano Roosevelt, invoked Paine's stirring words in a radio address on February 23, 1942. In one of his most memorable "fireside chats" to rally the nation's support for the war effort, FDR concluded by drawing on two of Paine's most celebrated passages. "'These are the times that try men's souls,'" he declared. "Tom Paine wrote those words on a drumhead, by the light of a campfire. That was when Washington's little army of ragged, rugged men was retreating across New Jersey, having tasted naught but defeat." Building on that fighting spirit, the President added:

> General Washington ordered that these great words written by Tom Paine be read to the men of every regiment in the Continental Army, and this was the assurance given to the first American armed forces: "The summer soldier and the sunshine patriot will, in this crisis, shrink from the service of their country; but he that stands it now, deserves the love and thanks of man and woman."

During the campaign to end the reign of Nazi conquest, squadrons of U.S. fighter planes known as the Flying Fortress took the war to the enemy's backyard. One of those bombers, a B-17F, was named "Tom Paine." The sides of the plane proudly proclaimed Paine's fighting message to the world: "Tyranny, like Hell, is not easily conquered!" The dead dissident had found his way back into the hearts of his fellow Americans.

Thomas Paine would likely have understood the fall and rise of his reputation. Indeed, he might have predicted it. For the opening words of his greatest work, *Common Sense*, revealed both his pessimism and optimism concerning the fate of a dissenter:

> Perhaps the sentiments contained in the following pages are not *yet* sufficiently fashionable to procure them general favor; a long habit of not thinking a thing *wrong*, gives it a superficial appearance of being *right*, and raises at first a formidable

outcry in defence of custom. But the tumult soon subsides.
Time makes more converts than reason.

The legacy of Thomas Paine teaches us important
lessons. Sedition can be the best test of loyalty. Heresy can be
the truest expression of faith. And dissent can be the highest form of patriotism. Our mission in this book has been
to sketch out the various ways in which these assertions
might be given credence. What is at stake here is not only
the sanctity of individual conscience but also the integrity
of our system of constitutional government.

CR SO

Consent and dissent are two sides of the same coin. Without dissent, consent is meaningless; without consent, dissent loses much of its animating purpose. In a truly robust
democracy, consent is the hard-earned end product of a
clash of views, of a full-bodied give-and-take in which the
dissenting message is permitted if only because it might –
against all odds – persuade others to heed its creed. "Consent," Paul Toscano reminds us, "draws its power from the
possibility of dissent." This is a lesson of both political theory and constitutional law. By this measure, dissent is not
a privilege granted by the powerful many to the powerless
few; it is a practice honored by the polity because our society cannot thrive without it. It is what legitimates democratic
governance; it is the seal affixed to the social contract.

If the Federalists of 1787 had their way, and if the First
Amendment were never added to the Constitution, it would

have been necessary to invent that great bulwark of freedom by implication. For without the liberty of the First Amendment, it would have been impossible to secure the free and open dissent vital to any system of government worthy of the name of democracy. If anything, the election of 1800, which ended the era of Federalist censorship under the Alien and Sedition Acts, brought that lesson home to our young nation. Mindful of this, Stephen Carter tellingly observes that our democracy depends on "the dissent of the governed." Indeed.

Dissent – whether lawful or otherwise – renders a great service to our system of constitutional and representative democracy and to the liberties integral to that way of political life. Salt Lake City attorney Paul Toscano, who knows firsthand the costs of dissent,* draws our attention to the quintessential work that dissent does to validate democracy and invigorate liberty:

- "It is the backbone of individual freedom."
- "It is the root of personal responsibility and spiritual maturation."
- "It is an antidote to idolatry."
- "It gives sight to the blind," and "can also heal institutional blindness."
- "It is the foundation of peace."
- And it tests, time and again, "the wisdom of the majority."

---

* According to news reports from the time, Toscano was excommunicated by Mormon Church officials in September 1993 for criticizing certain alterations in church teachings and for what he perceived to be oppressive church leadership.

In these ways and others, dissent works to preserve our democratic system. It is loyal to that ideal; it is faithful to that principle; and it is therefore skeptical of those who hold that democracy is so perfect that there is no more room for different opinions. While dissenters may well be heretics in the herd, they nonetheless remind us that herd mentality is contrary to the spirit of a freethinking and freedom-loving people. They goad us even when we savor the stupor of our own folly.

There is a man who has stood outside the Vatican Embassy (or The Apostolic Nunciature, as it is officially known) for nearly every day for the past fifteen years. Passersby see him at his post, in snow or sun, armed with this or that sign of protest. Some banners scream out in bold black and red letters: "VATICAN AIDS PEDOPHILES" and "POPE SODOMIZES JUSTICE." Other banners are cast in white and yellow: "CATHOLIC COWARDS." The anti-pedophile activist on the Washington, DC sidewalk, the dissident behind the signs, is John Wojnowski. This white-haired 70-year-old man has proclaimed his dissent for 5,000-plus days. His persistent outspokenness is, to say the least, unwelcomed by those behind the forbidding doors in front of which he preaches his gospel of protest. Are his rants true? Are his criticisms fair? Are his accusations over the top? Perhaps. Perhaps not. Either way, there is something magnificent in beholding such a sight in our nation's capital. It is a sign of dissent – which is a good sign in a democracy.

NOTES

Prologue

- Re dictionary definition of dissent: "Dissent" in Lesley Brown, editor, *The New Shorter Oxford English Dictionary* (New York: Oxford University Press, 1993), 1: 702 (second definition).

From Judicial Dissent to Peaceful Protest

- Re *Abrams v. United States*: 250 U.S. 616, 624, 630 (1919) (Holmes, J., dissenting).
- Re Port Huron Statement: Tom Hayden, *The Port Huron Statement: The Visionary Call of the 1960s Revolution* (New York: Thunder's Mouth Press, 2005), pp. 1–48.
- Re *Dissent in America*: Ralph F. Young, editor, *Dissent in America: The Voices That Shaped a Nation* (New York: Longman, 2009).
- Re *Texas v. Johnson*: 491 U.S. 397, 403 n. 3 (1989).
- Re dictionary definition of dissent: "Dissent" in Lesley Brown, editor, *The New Shorter Oxford English Dictionary* (New York: Oxford University Press, 1993), 1: 702 (second definition).
- Re Luther: H. G. Haile, *Luther: An Experiment in Biography* (Princeton, NJ: Princeton University Press, 1983), pp. 205–258.
- Re John Doe hypothetical: This scenario derives loosely from the Dennis R. Beller story. Joyce Murdoch and Deb Price, *Courting Justice: Gay Men and Lesbians v. the Supreme Court* (New York: Basic Books, 2001), pp. 208–212; *Beller v. Lehman*, 632 F.2d 792 (9th Cir., 1980).

- Re anti-miscegenation: *Loving v. Virginia*, 388 U.S. 1 (1967); Pippa Holloway, *Sexuality, Politics, and Social Control in Virginia, 1920–1945* (Chapel Hill: University of North Carolina Press, 2007).
- Re King essay: Martin Luther King, "A Testament of Hope," in James M. Washington, editor, *A Testament of Hope: The Essential Writings of Martin Luther King, Jr.* (New York: Harper & Row, 1986), pp. 327–328.
- Re *Ruthenberg v. Michigan*: Ronald K. L. Collins and David M. Skover, "Curious Concurrence: Justice Brandeis's Vote in *Whitney v. California*," *The Supreme Court Review* 2005: 333, 388–395. See also Alexander M. Bickel, *The Unpublished Opinions of Mr. Justice Brandeis: The Supreme Court at Work* (Cambridge, MA: Harvard University Press, 1957).
- Re esoteric dissent: Leo Strauss, *Persecution and the Art of Writing* (New York: The Free Press, 1952), pp. 23, 24, 33.
- Re anonymous publications: *Talley v. California*, 362 U.S. 60, 64–65 (1960).

From Civil to Uncivil Disobedience

- Re Aldyn McKean: Ralph F. Young, editor, *Dissent in America: The Voices That Shaped a Nation* (New York: Longman, 2009), p. 681.
- Re Muhammad Ali: Thomas Hauser, *Muhammad Ali: His Life and Times* (New York: Simon and Schuster, 1992), pp. 145–202.
- Re Thoreau: Young, *Dissent in America*, pp. 211–228; Owen Thomas, editor, *Walden and Civil Disobedience* (New York: W. W. Norton & Co., 1966).
- Re "civil disobedience is not dissent, but merely an illegal act": This perspective is ably described and explored in Brent R. Cromley, "The Right to Dissent in a Free Society," *Montana Law Review* 32: 215, 223–225 (1971) (a "free society" can only

tolerate a highly restricted recognition of civil disobedience as a right to dissent, since even nonviolent transgression of law "encourages a general disrespect for law and order," tends to "escalate" to more violent action, and "is not susceptible to principles of general application").

- Re ACT-UP. Deborah B. Gould, *Moving Politics: Emotion and Act-Up's Fight against AIDS* (Chicago: University of Chicago Press, 2009), pp. 290–292.
- Re César Chávez: Jacques E. Levy, *César Chávez: Autobiography of La Causa* (Minneapolis: University of Minnesota Press, 2007), pp. 206–214.
- Re Eugene Debs: Nick Salvatore, *Eugene V. Debs: Citizen & Socialist* (Champaign: University of Illinois Press, 1984), p. 291. The text of the speech can be found in Young, *Dissent in America*, pp. 411–416.
- Re in-group opposition: One of our commentators, Michael Walzer, stressed in his own work the importance of "insider" status for effective criticism: "[C]riticism is most properly the work of 'insiders,' men and women mindful of and committed to the society whose policies or practices they call into question. . . . The ideal critic is part of his or her society, engaged rather than detached." Michael Walzer, *The Company of Critics* (New York: Basic Books, 2002), pp. xi–xii.

The Vagaries of Violence

- Re definition of "violence": Lesley Brown, editor, *The New Shorter Oxford English Dictionary* (New York: Oxford University Press, 1993), 2: 3585.
- Re Cantonsville Nine: "Nine Seize and Burn 600 Draft Files," *New York Times*, May 18, 1968, p. 36; Spencer C. Tucker, editor, *The Encyclopedia of the Vietnam War* (Santa Barbara, CA: ABC-CLIO, 2011), p. 178; Anne Klejmant, "War Resistance and Property Destruction: The Cantonsville Nine Draft

Board Raid and Catholic Worker Pacifism," in Patrick G. Coy, editor, *A Revolution of the Heart* (Philadelphia: Temple University Press, 1988), pp. 272, 277; see generally Daniel Berrigan, *The Trial of Cantonsville Nine* (New York: Fordham University Press, 2004).

• Re Gail Shea pie-throwing: John Burman and Mark McNeil, "Anti-Sealing PETA Protester Smacks Minister with Tofu Pie," *The Hamilton Spectator*, January 25, 2010; "Pie-Tossing Is Terrorism, MP Says," *Toronto Star*, January 26, 2010.

• Re Lincoln assassination: James Swanson, *Manhunt: The 12-Day Chase for Lincoln's Killer* (New York: HarperCollins, 2006), pp. 35–94.

• Re Unabomber: Theodore J. Kaczynski, *Technological Slavery: The Collected Writings of Theodore J. Kaczynski, a.k.a. "The Unabomber"* (Port Townsend, WA: Feral House, 2010), pp. 38–39; Ralph F. Young, editor, *Dissent in America: The Voices That Shaped a Nation* (New York: Longman, 2009), pp. 437–438.

• Re Supreme Court civil rights cases: *Griffin v. Maryland*, 378 U.S. 130 (1964) (invalidating arrest for criminal trespass in a racially segregated public park on Fourteenth Amendment equal protection grounds); *NAACP v. Claiborne Hardware Company*, 458 U.S. 886 (1982) (setting aside on First Amendment grounds a civil damages award arising out of a civil-rights economic boycott with some violent overtones); *New York Times v. Sullivan*, 376 U.S. 254 (1964) (recognizing First Amendment press rights to defame public officials). See also *Edwards v. South Carolina*, 372 U.S. 229 (1963) (upholding First Amendment rights of assembly and petition on state house grounds); *Brown v. Louisiana*, 383 U.S. 131 (1966) (library sit-in arrest invalidated on First and Fourteenth Amendment grounds).

• Re John Lennon: Albert Goldman, *The Lives of John Lennon* (New York: William Morrow & Co., 1988), pp. 684–687.

• Re in-group opposition and revolution: In a related way, sociologist Herbert Blumer distinguished a reform movement (i.e., "to change some specific phase or limited area of the existing social order") from a revolutionary movement (i.e., "to reconstruct the entire social order"). See Herbert Blumer, "Social Movements," in *The Sociology of Dissent*, edited by R. Serge Denisoff (New York: Harcourt Brace Jovanovich, 1974), p. 14.

- Re Michael Griffin: Judy Mann, "Terrorism at the Clinics," *Washington Post*, March 12, 1993, sec. E, p. 3.
- Re Bank of America burning: CBS National News with Walter Cronkite, February 26, 1970, www.youtube.com/watch?v=NX8WCEtoDZM; "Archives: ISLA Vista Student Riots (1970)," www.hippy.com/modules.php?name=News&file=article&sid=173; Lou Cannon, *Governor Reagan: His Rise to Power* (New York: PublicAffairs, 2003), pp. 293–294; James F. Short, Jr. and Marvin E. Wolfgang, editors, *Collective Violence in the United States* (New Brunswick, NJ: Transaction Publishers, 2009), p. 269.
- Re relative powerlessness and numerical minority status: For an interesting account of the notion of "dissenting by deciding," a phenomenon that "occurs when would-be dissenters – individuals who hold a minority view within the polity as a whole – enjoy a local majority on a decisionmaking body and can thus dictate the outcome," see Heather K. Gerken, "Dissenting by Deciding," *Stanford Law Review* 47: 1745 (2005).
- Re acknowledgment of the rule of law, acceptance of punishment, and the "spirit of Socratic honor": For a strong statement of the importance of this attribute to any meaningful notion of dissent, particularly in the arena of civil disobedience, see Abe Fortas, *Concerning Dissent and Civil Disobedience* (New York: Signet Books, 1968), pp. 63–64 ("[E]ach of us must be ready, like Socrates, to accept the verdict of [society's] institutions if we violate their mandate and our challenge is not vindicated. . . . [Dissenters] must accept dissent from their dissent. . . . Protest does not justify hooliganism.").

- Re Idi Amin: John Allen, *Idi Amin* (Farmington Hills, MI: Blackbirch Press, 2003).

Dissent, Inc.

- The scenarios we use in this chapter are a combination of fact and fiction. Although they reflect something of the spirit of the times, they are not always true to any particular historical account. The same is the case for the "laws" and parties to which we refer within the scenarios.
- Re Jehovah's Witnesses: This example is loosely patterned after *Marsh v. Alabama*, 326 U.S. 501 (1946) and *Marsh v. State*, 21 So. 2d 558 (Ala. App. 1945). See generally Shawn Francis Peters, *Judging Jehovah's Witnesses: Religious Prosecution and the Dawn of the Rights Revolution* (Lawrence: University Press of Kansas, 2002).
- Re HUAC: This example is creatively derived from the history of the House Un-American Activities Committee hearings in the 1950s and the subsequent and unrelated mandates of the 2002 Bipartisan Campaign Reform Act (commonly known as the McCain-Feingold Act) at the center of the Supreme Court's ruling in *Citizens United v. Federal Election Commission*, 558 U.S. 50 (2010).
- Re economic boycott: This example derives from *NAACP v. Claiborne Hardware Co.*, 393 So. 2d 1290 (Miss. 1980) and *NAACP v. Claiborne Hardware Co.*, 458 U.S. 886 (1982). See also Emilye Crosby, *A Little Taste of Freedom: The Black Freedom Struggle in Claiborne County, Mississippi* (Durham: University of North Carolina Press, 2005).
- Re 185 years: The extension of constitutional protection to commercial messages by corporations occurred in *Virginia State Board of Pharmacy v. Virginia Citizens Consumer Council, Inc.*, 425 U.S. 748 (1976). See also *44 Liquormart, Inc. v. Rhode Island*, 517 U.S. 484 (1996).

- Re footnote reference to Catharine MacKinnon: A similar argument that First Amendment protection of Ku Klux Klan "hate speakers" conflicts with a notion of dissent, properly understood, is made in Steven H. Shiffrin, *Dissent, Injustice, and the Meanings of America* (Princeton, NJ: Princeton University Press, 1999), pp. 76–77 ("Although vocal proponents of racism are a minority group despised by many, they also state aloud views that are widely though privately held in society. . . . [Race] continues to be used as a means of perpetuating inequality, [and] the initiator of racist speech further aggravates the position of the subordinated.").
- Re footnote reference to Supreme Court holding: *Brandenburg v. Ohio*, 395 U.S. 444 (1969).
- Re footnote on pornography: See Ronald Collins and David Skover, *The Death of Discourse* (Durham, NC: Carolina Academic Press, 2nd ed. 2005), pp. 142–147.
- Re Che Guevara: See Michael J. Casey, *Che's Afterlife: The Legacy of an Image* (New York: Vintage, 2009).
- Re "parasitic class": Che Guevara, *Guerilla Warfare* (Omaha: University of Nebraska Press, 1998), p. 123.

Dissent and Law's Parameters

- Re Justice Louis Brandeis: *Whitney v. California*, 247 U.S. 357, 375 (1927) (Brandeis, J., concurring).
- Re Benjamin Bache: Jeffrey A. Smith, *Franklin & Bache: Envisioning the Enlightened Republic* (New York: Oxford University Press, 1990); James Tagg, *Benjamin Franklin Bache and the Philadelphia Aurora* (Philadelphia: University of Pennsylvania Press, 1991); Peter Charles Hoffer, *The Free Press Crisis of 1800* (Lawrence: University Press of Kansas, 2011); James Morton Smith, *Freedom's Fetters: The Alien and Sedition Laws and American Civil Liberties* (Ithaca, NY: Cornell University Press, 1956).
- Re Sedition Act: "An Act for the Punishment of Certain Crimes against the United States," ch.74, 1 Stat. 596.

- Re "declared war on dissent": Geoffrey Stone, *Perilous Times: Free Speech in Wartime* (New York: W. W. Norton & Co., 2004), p. 36.
- Re Justice William Brennan: *New York Times v. Sullivan*, 376 U.S. 254, 276 (1964).
- Re Justice William O. Douglas: William O. Douglas, *Points of Rebellion* (New York: Random House, 1969), p. 3. In fairness to Douglas, the remainder of the text does provide greater illumination as to the scope of his statement. Nonetheless, the reader must work mightily to discern the precise parameters of what Douglas understands dissent to be and whether such dissent could ever be protected by the First Amendment. See *id.* at 4–6 and 88–89 ("Violence has no constitutional sanction.... But where grievances pile high and most of the elected spokesmen represent the Establishment, violence may be the only effective response.").
- Re Camus: Albert Camus, *Resistance, Rebellion, and Death*, translated by Justin O'Brien (New York: Alfred Knopf, 1961), p. 5 (referring to Germany's unconscionable excesses during the Second World War).
- Re anti-abolitionist statutes: Michael Kent Curtis, *Free Speech, "The People's Darling Privilege"* (Durham, NC: Duke University Press, 2000), pp. 136–138; "An Act to Prevent the Circulation of Seditious Pamphlets, Papers, and Magazines," §§1–5, *Laws of the State of Mississippi 1824–1838* (Baltimore: John D. Toy, 1838), pp. 328–330; see also Ford Risley, *Abolition and the Press: The Moral Struggle against Slavery* (Chicago: Northwestern University Press, 2008), p. 44 (laws of Virginia and other Southern states); Christopher B. Daly, *Covering America: A Narrative History of a Nation's Journalism* (Boston: University of Massachusetts Press, 2012), p. 95.
- Re Wobblies: Stephen M. Feldman, *Free Expression and Democracy in America: A History* (Chicago: University of Chicago Press, 2008), pp. 230–231.

- Re Women's Suffrage: Jarret S. Lovell, *Crimes of Dissent: Civil Disobedience, Criminal Justice, and the Politics of Conscience* (New York: New York University Press, 2009), p. 9.
- Re Red Scare: Geoffrey R. Stone, *Perilous Times: Free Speech in Wartime* (New York: W. W. Norton & Co., 2004), p. 224.
- Re "liberty by permission": Theodore Schroeder, *Free Speech for Radicals* (New York: Burt Franklin, 1916), pp. 1, 84.
- Re Benjamin Franklin: Bryan-Paul Frost and Jeffrey Sikkenga, editors, *History of American Political Thought* (Lanham, MD: Lexington Books, 2003), p. 385.
- Re bulleted claims of "right" protected under the First Amendment: *New York Times Co. v. Sullivan*, 376 U.S. 254 (1964) (defamation); *Hustler Magazine v. Falwell*, 485 U.S. 46 (1988) (privacy and intentional infliction of emotional distress); *NAACP v. Claiborne Hardware Co.*, 458 U.S. 886 (1982) (economic boycott of commercial business); *Tinker v. Des Moines Independent Community School District*, 393 U.S. 503 (1969) (school rules); *West Virginia State Board of Education v. Barnette*, 319 U.S. 624 (1943) (school policies); *Marsh v. Alabama*, 326 U.S. 501 (1946) (trespass on private property); *Grayned v. City of Rockford*, 408 U.S. 104 (1972) (anti-noise ordinance); *Cohen v. California*, 403 U.S. 15 (1971) (vulgarities in courthouse); *Thornhill v. Alabama*, 310 U.S. 88 (1940) (loitering and picketing); *De Jonge v. Oregon*, 299 U.S. 353 (1937) (disorderly conduct); *Hague v. CIO*, 307 U.S. 496 (1939) (disorderly conduct); *Cox v. Louisiana*, 379 U.S. 536 (1956) (breach of the peace); *Edwards v. South Carolina*, 372 U.S. 229 (1963) (breach of the peace); *Brown v. Louisiana*, 383 U.S. 131 (1966) (breach of the peace); *Brandenburg v. Ohio*, 395 U.S. 444 (1969) (advocacy of illegal action).
- Re "political speech is central": *Citizens United v. Federal Election Commission*, 130 S. Ct. 876, 892 (2010).
- Re "political speech is the primary object": *Federal Election Commission v. Colorado Republican Federal Campaign*

*Comm*ission, 533 U.S. 431, 488 (2001) (Thomas, J., dissenting).

- Re "First Amendment requires": *Federal Election Commission v. Wisconsin Right to Life, Inc.*, 551 U.S. 449, 457 (2007).
- Re "regulate core political speech": *Davis v. Federal Election Commission*, 554 U.S. 724, 754 (2008).
- Re dissent as central to any notion of political speech: In this regard, Professor Steven Shiffrin astutely observes: "If we must have a 'central meaning' of the First Amendment, we should recognize that the dissenters – those who attack existing customs, habits, traditions, and authorities – stand at the center of the First Amendment, and not its periphery. . . . The First Amendment has a special regard for those who swim against the current, for those who would shake us to our foundations, for those who reject prevailing authority." Steven H. Shiffrin, *Dissent, Injustice, and the Meanings of America* (Princeton, NJ: Princeton University Press, 1999), p. 10. Strictly speaking, Shiffrin does not explicitly make our point that political speech lies at the core of the First Amendment, and dissent is central to any meaningful notion of political speech; certainly, however, his argument implicitly supports it.
- Re Abraham Lincoln: Joe Wheeler, *Abraham Lincoln: A Man of Faith and Courage* (New York: Simon & Schuster, 2008), p. 294.
- Re Martin Luther King: Martin Luther King, Letter from the Birmingham Jail, in James M. Washington, editor, *A Testament of Hope: The Essential Writings of Martin Luther King, Jr.* (San Francisco, CA: Harper & Row, 1986), pp. 289–302.
- Re Christopher Hitchins: Christopher Hitchins, *Letters to a Young Contrarian* (New York: Basic Books, 2005), p. 33.
- Re First Amendment and Student Rights: *Tinker v. Des Moines Independent Community School District*, 393 U.S. 503 (1969); Scott A. Moss, "The Story of *Tinker v. Des Moines* to *Morse v. Frederick*: Similar Stories of Different Student Speech with

Different Results," in Richard W. Garnett and Andrew Koppelman, editors, *First Amendment Stories* (New York: Foundation Press, 2012), pp. 401–410; Ronald K. L. Collins and Sam Chaltain, *We Must Not Be Afraid to Be Free: Stories of Free Expression in America* (New York: Oxford University Press, 2011), pp. 270–284.

- Re "no First Amendment problem": Del Dickson, editor, *The Supreme Court in Conference (1940–1985)* (New York: Oxford University Press, 2001), p. 338 (conference notes of November 15, 1968).
- Re First Amendment and Defamation: Anthony Lewis, *Make No Law: The Sullivan Case and the First Amendment* (New York: Random House, 1991); Kermit L. Hall and Melvin I. Urofsky, *New York Times v. Sullivan: Civil Rights, Libel Law, and the Free Press* (Lawrence: University Press of Kansas, 2011).
- Re Anthony Lewis and Alexander Meiklejohn: Lewis, *Make No Law*, p. 154.
- Re Alexander Bickel: Alexander M. Bickel, *The Morality of Consent* (New Haven, CT: Yale University Press, 1975), p. 57.
- Re "Justice Brennan widely redrew": Hall and Urofsky, *New York Times v. Sullivan*, p. 202.
- Re First Amendment and Advocacy of Illegal Action: *Brandenburg v. Ohio*, 395 U.S. 444, 447 (1969); Collins and Chaltain, *We Must Not Be Afraid to Be Free*, pp. 167–168; Ronald K. L. Collins, editor, *The Fundamental Holmes: A Free Speech Chronicle and Reader* (New York: Cambridge University Press, 2010), pp. 363–367 (law of incitement prior to *Brandenburg*); Richard A. Parker, editor, *Free Speech on Trial: Communication Perspectives on Landmark Supreme Court Decisions* (Tuscaloosa: University of Alabama Press, 2003), pp. 146–156 (precedents before *Brandenburg*, analysis of *Brandenburg* opinion, and discussion of *Brandenburg*'s influence in criminal and civil law contexts).
- Re Oliver Wendell Holmes, Jr.: *United States v. Schwimmer*, 279 U.S. 644, 654–655 (1929) (Holmes, J., dissenting).

- Re footnote on substantial overbreadth doctrine: See, e.g., *Broadrick v. Oklahoma*, 413 U.S. 601 (1973) (articulating the governing standard for a First Amendment substantial overbreadth challenge); *Village of Hoffman Estates v. Flipside, Hoffman Estates Inc.*, 455 U.S. 489, 494–95 (1982) (recognizing that the analytical pathways for vagueness and substantial overbreadth claims are intertwined); *Gooding v. Wilson*, 405 U.S. 518 (1972) (invalidating the criminal conviction of a Vietnam War protestor, who cursed police officers during a demonstration, under an unconstitutionally overbroad state statute that prohibited "opprobrious words or abusive language, tending to cause a breach of the peace"); *Alabama Education Association v. Bentley*, 788 F. Supp. 2d 1283 (N.D. Ala. 2011) (issuing a preliminary injunction against enforcement of an Alabama criminal statute that prohibited any state or local government employee from "arranging by salary deduction or otherwise" for payments to political action committees or any membership organizations involved in "political activities," on the basis that the plaintiffs had established a substantial likelihood of success on the merits of their excessive vagueness and substantial overbreadth claims, among others).
- Re void-for-vagueness doctrine: See, e.g., *Forsyth County v. Nationalist Movement*, 505 U.S. 123 (1992) (in the context of a proposed demonstration to oppose the federal holiday commemorating the birthday of Martin Luther King, Jr., a county ordinance authorizing administrative officials to impose permit fees for private demonstrations in public places was invalidated as unconstitutionally vague on its face for failing to establish definite standards that narrowly constrained administrative discretion in fee-setting); *Coates v. Cincinnati*, 402 U.S. 611 (1971) (overturning the criminal convictions of a student demonstrator and of picketers involved in a labor dispute for violations of a Cincinnati ordinance, deemed unconstitutionally vague, that prohibited any assembly on a public sidewalk in

a fashion that annoys passersby); *Baggett v. Bullitt*, 377 U.S. 360 (1964) (invalidating as unconstitutionally vague a state statute requiring teachers and other governmental employees to take loyalty oaths, swearing to reverence for law and order, pledging allegiance to constituted government, and denying any "subversive" activity, including the teaching or advocating of any action to overthrow or alter the government by revolution, force, or violence).

- Re description of the necessity defense: William P. Quigley, "The Necessity Defense in Civil Obedience Cases: Bring in the Jury," *New England Law Review* 38: 3, 13, 26 (2003).
- Re waxing and waning of the necessity defense: Quigley, "The Necessity Defense in Civil Obedience Cases," pp. 26–37 (examples from 1977 to 1993 of state court criminal and civil cases in which the necessity defense was invoked and jury acquittal rendered); James L. Cavallaro, "The Demise of the Political Necessity Defense: Indirect Civil Disobedience and *United States v. Schoon*," *California Law Review* 81: 351, 360–361 (1993) ("In contrast with the federal courts' unwillingness to permit the necessity defense, civil disobedients in state courts have often invoked the defense and won acquittal. Defendants have successfully argued necessity in prosecutions based on protests against U.S. Central-American policy, nuclear power and weaponry, apartheid, and policies of the CIA."); Bernard Lambek, "Necessity and International Law: Arguments for the Loyalty of Civil Disobedience," *Yale Law & Policy Review* 5: 472, 473 (1986) ("When the necessity defense is actually submitted to the trier of fact in civil disobedience cases, defendants have usually been acquitted.").

Epilogue

- Re epigraph quotation: Christopher Hitchins, *Letters to a Young Contrarian* (New York, Basic Books, 2001), p. 1.

- Re "single most influential political work": Scott Liell, *46 Pages: Thomas Paine, Common Sense, and the Turning Point to Independence* (Philadelphia: Running Press, 2003), p. 16.
- Re George Washington: Liell, *46 Pages*, p. 113.
- Re "a rage and a fury": Thomas Paine, *Common Sense and Other Writings*, edited and introduced by Gordon S. Wood (New York: Modern Library, 2003), p. xxxiii.
- Re "did not merely change minds": Liell, *46 Pages*, p. 20.
- Re "no eulogies": Harvey J. Kaye, *Thomas Paine: Firebrand of the Revolution* (New York: Oxford University Press, 2000), p. 143.
- Re "I do not believe in the creed": Thomas Paine, "The Age of Reason," in Paine, *Common Sense and Other Writings*," p. 245.
- Re "unchristianize the mass of our citizens": Jerry R. Self, *America's God and Its Founding Fathers* (New York: Vantage Press, 2008), p. 85.
- Re "satyr" begotten by a "wild boar on a bitch wolf": David Freeman Hawke, *Paine* (New York: Harper & Row, 1974), p. 7.
- Re Theodore Roosevelt: Daniel Ruddy, editor, *Theodore Roosevelt's History of the United States: His Own Words* (New York: HarperCollins, 2010), p. 33.
- Re "fireside chat": Franklin D. Roosevelt, "Fireside Chat – February 23, 1942," in *The American Presidency Project*, www.presidency.ucsb.edu/ws/index.php?pid=16224.
- Re "These are the times" and "The summer soldier": Thomas Paine, *The American Crisis I*, in *The Life and Major Writings of Thomas Paine*, edited by Philip S. Foner (Secaucus, NJ: Citadel Press, 1948), p. 50.
- Re B-17F plane: Kaye, *Thomas Paine*, at 142. The quotation on the side of the plane came from Paine's *American Crisis I*.
- Re "Perhaps the sentiments contained": *The Life and Major Writings*, p. 3.
- Re Paul Toscano: Paul Toscano, "The Sanctity of Dissent," in Stephen P. Banks, editor, *Dissent and the Failure of Leadership* (Northampton, MA: Edward Elgar Publishing, 2008), p. 170.

- Re Stephen Carter: Stephen L. Carter, *The Dissent of the Governed: A Meditation on Law, Religion, and Loyalty* (Cambridge, MA: Harvard University Press, 1998), p. 97.
- Re "the quintessential work" of dissent: Toscano, "The Sanctity of Dissent," pp. 170–177.
- Re footnote on Paul Toscano. Dirk Johnson, "As Mormon Church Grows, So Does Dissent from Feminists and Scholars," *New York Times*, October 2, 1993, sec. 1, p. 7; Paul Toscano, telephonic interview by authors, July 22, 2012, Bethesda, Maryland (footnote statement confirmed by Toscano).
- Re John Wojnowski: Ariel Sabar, "The Passion of John Wojnowski," *The Washingtonian*, June 25, 2012.

ACKNOWLEDGMENTS

This book has been in gestation for several years. During that period, we have been the beneficiaries of the goodwill of many individuals, particularly our *Informationis Personae* who thoughtfully engaged us in the give-and-take of dialogue. It is reassuring to know that, in today's world, the love of ideas is still cherished and genuine and profound intellectual exchange is still possible. There is something old-fashioned about all of this: real people meeting face-to-face in real time to hammer out real answers to difficult questions, and thereby contributing to the bounty of public knowledge.

Given its long-standing commitment to scholarship, Cambridge University Press was the ideal publisher for this project. And John Berger was our ideal editor. From the outset, he believed in this book and shepherded it to completion. John's dedication to serious works of legal thought is something of an anomaly in an era in which too many academic publishers have abased their once lofty intellectual purposes in favor of mere entrepreneurial profits.

Dean Kellye Testy of the University of Washington School of Law and Dean Mark Niles of Seattle University School of Law were generous in their financial support of the research and writing of this book. This project would have been impossible without them.

Special appreciation goes to Nancy Harrop, our tireless administrative assistant who has worked with us for thirty-some years; to Kelly Kunsch, our able research librarian who has, for decades, pointed us in the right directions; to Jennifer Lim, who accurately transcribed the many and long interviews conducted for this book; and to Albert Kang and Elena Oguiza, who diligently assisted in creating the Index.

Once again, we lovingly express our sincere gratitude to Susan A. Cohen, who provided behind-the-scenes advice and encouragement with grace and good humor.

Ron Collins: My thanks to Linda Hopkins, a mainstay of needed support that empowered my writing, both present and future.

David Skover: My thanks to my immediate family and my extended family of faithful friends who applauded me on sunny days and uplifted me in darker times.

We raise our cups to them all . . . *without dissent!*

ABOUT THE AUTHORS

Ronald K.L. Collins is the Harold S. Shefelman Scholar at the University of Washington Law School. Before coming to the Law School, Collins served as a law clerk to Justice Hans A. Linde on the Oregon Supreme Court, a Supreme Court Fellow under Chief Justice Warren Burger, and a scholar at the Washington, DC office of the First Amendment Center, where he wrote and lectured on freedom of expression and oversaw the online library component of the First Amendment Center's Web site.

Collins has taught constitutional law and contract law at Temple Law School, George Washington Law School, Seattle University School of Law, and the University of Washington Law School. He has written constitutional briefs that were submitted to the Supreme Court and various other federal and state high courts. His journalistic writings on the First Amendment have appeared in *Columbia Journalism Review*, *New York Times*, and *The Washington Post*, among other publications. He is the book editor of SCOTUSblog. In addition to the books that he coauthored with David Skover, Ron is the editor of *Oliver Wendell Holmes: A Free Speech Chronicle and Reader* (Cambridge University Press, 2010) and coauthor, with Sam Chaltain, of *We Must Not Be Afraid to Be Free* (2011). His latest book is *Nuanced Absolutism: Floyd Abrams and the First Amendment* (2012).

David M. Skover is the Fredric C. Tausend Professor of Law at Seattle University School of Law. He teaches, writes, and lectures in the fields of federal constitutional law, federal jurisdiction, mass communications theory, and the First Amendment.

David graduated from the Woodrow Wilson School of International and Domestic Affairs at Princeton University. He received his law degree from Yale Law School, where he was an editor of the *Yale Law Journal.* Thereafter, he served as a law clerk for Judge Jon O. Newman of the U.S. Court of Appeals for the Second Circuit. In addition to the books that he coauthored with Ronald Collins, David is the coauthor, with Pierre Schlag, of *Tactics of Legal Reasoning* (1986).

ഔ ഇ

Collins and Skover have coauthored three other books: *The Death of Discourse* (1996; 2nd edition 2005) (*Publishers Weekly* star review), *The Trials of Lenny Bruce* (2002; expanded e-book version 2012) (*Los Angeles Times* selection for "Best Book of the Year"), and *Mania: The Story of the Outraged and Outrageous Lives That Launched a Generation* (2013). Moreover, they have coauthored dozens of scholarly articles in various journals, including *The Supreme Court Review, Harvard Law Review, Stanford Law Review, Michigan Law Review, Texas Law Review, The Nation* magazine, and the *Yale Bibliographical Dictionary of American Law.* Their latest essays are "The Digital Path of the Law," in Edward Rubin, editor, *Legal Education in the Digital Age* (Cambridge University Press, 2012), and "Foreword: The Guardians of Truth in the Modern State: Post's Republic and the First Amendment," *Washington Law Review* (2012).

In 2003, Collins and Skover successfully petitioned the governor of New York to posthumously pardon Lenny Bruce. In 2004, they received the Hugh Hefner First Amendment Award for *The Trials of Lenny Bruce* and their pardon effort. Together and individually, Collins and Skover have appeared frequently on network affiliate television, have been heard often on radio interviews, and have been quoted in the national popular press on a spectrum of issues ranging from First Amendment and constitutional law to popular media culture and theory.

ABOUT THE INFORMATIONIS PERSONAE

Randy E. Barnett is the Carmack Waterhouse Professor of Legal Theory at the Georgetown University Law Center in Washington, DC. He teaches and writes in the areas of constitutional law and contracts, and is known as a libertarian theorist.

Noam Chomsky is an Institute Professor and a professor in the Department of Linguistics and Philosophy in the Massachusetts Institute of Technology in Cambridge, MA. He is recognized as a linguist, philosopher, cognitive scientist, historian, and political activist.

Phil Donahue is a media personality, writer, and film producer. Best known as the creator and host of the first talk-show television program, *The Phil Donahue Show*, he focused on highly controversial and politically divisive social issues, such as abortion, civil rights, and war.

Todd Gitlin is a professor in the School of Journalism at Columbia University in New York. His areas of teaching and scholarship include mass communications theory and cultural sociology.

Steven K. Green is the Fred H. Paulus Professor of Law and the Director of the Center for Religion, Law, and Democracy at Willamette in Salem, OR. He teaches and writes in the areas of constitutional law, First Amendment law, legal history, administrative law, and criminal law.

Kent Greenawalt is a University Professor at Columbia Law School in New York. His primary scholarly and teaching interests involve constitutional law, especially First Amendment jurisprudence, and legal philosophy.

Sue Curry Jansen is a Professor in the Media and Communications Department of Muhlenberg College in Allentown, PA. Her teaching and writing focus on issues of freedom of expression broadly conceived, including relationships of power to knowledge.

Sut Jhally is a Professor of Communication at the University of Massachusetts at Amherst. He is a leading expert on cultural studies, media and advertising, and consumption.

Anita K. Krug is a professor at the University of Washington School of Law in Seattle, WA. She teaches business and securities law courses, and writes primarily in the area of securities regulation.

Hans A. Linde is a former professor at the University of Oregon School of Law in Eugene and an Oregon Supreme Court Justice. He currently is a distinguished scholar in residence at Willamette University College of Law. His writings focus primarily on federal and state constitutional law issues.

Catharine A. MacKinnon is the Elizabeth A. Long Professor of Law at the University of Michigan Law School in Ann Arbor, MI. Her teaching and writing center on sex equality issues under international and constitutional law.

Ralph Nader is a political activist, as well as an author and lecturer. His areas of particular concern include consumer protection, environmentalism, and democratic government.

Jon O. Newman is a federal judge who has served on the U.S. Court of Appeals for the Second Circuit since 1979. His best known opinion, written as a federal district court judge in 1972, invalidated Connecticut's abortion statute, a decision viewed as the precursor to the U.S. Supreme Court's decision in *Roe v. Wade* the following year.

Martha C. Nussbaum is the Ernst Freund Distinguished Service Professor of Law and Ethics, who teaches in the Department of Philosophy and in the Law School at the University of Chicago. A philosopher with a particular interest in ancient Greek and Roman philosophy, her teaching and writing focus on political philosophy, feminism, and ethics, including animal rights.

Frederick Schauer is the David and Mary Harrison Distinguished Professor of Law at the University of Virginia School of Law in Charlottesville, VA. He teaches and writes on constitutional law and theory, freedom of speech and press, legal reasoning, and the philosophy of law.

Steven H. Shiffrin is the Charles Frank Reavis, Sr. Professor of Law at Cornell Law School in Ithaca, NY. His teaching and writing interests center on constitutional law issues, with a special focus on First Amendment speech and religion topics, including dissent.

Faith Stevelman is a Professor of Law and Director of the Center on Business Law and Policy at New York Law School in New York City. She is an authority on corporate governance and securities law.

Geoffrey R. Stone is the Edward H. Levi Distinguished Service Professor at the University of Chicago School of Law. He teaches primarily in the areas of constitutional law and evidence, and writes principally in the field of constitutional law, with a particular focus on First Amendment issues.

Nadine Strossen is a professor at New York Law School and the former national president of the American Civil Liberties Union. She has written, lectured, and practiced extensively in the areas of constitutional law, civil liberties, and international human rights.

Michael Walzer is a professor emeritus at the Institute for Advanced Study in Princeton, NJ. A coeditor of *Dissent* magazine and a contributing editor to *The New Republic*, he has written books and essays on a wide range of topics, including just and unjust wars, nationalism, ethnicity, economic justice, social criticism and radicalism, and political obligations.

Cornel West is a professor of African-American studies at Princeton University in Princeton, NJ, and of religious philosophy at the Union Theological Seminary in New

York City. As a philosopher, author, civil rights activist, and prominent member of the Democratic Socialists of America, he focuses primarily on the roles of race, gender, and class in American society.

Howard Zinn was an American historian, academic, author, playwright, and social activist. Before and during his tenure as a political science professor at Boston University from 1964 to 1988, he wrote more than twenty books focusing on the civil rights, antiwar, and labor movements in the United States.

SELECT AND ANNOTATED BIBLIOGRAPHY

The *interviews* conducted for *On Dissent* include:

Barnett, Randy E. Interview by Ronald Collins and David Skover. Tape recording, June 2, 2012. Washington, DC.

Chomsky, Noam. Interview by David Skover. Tape recording, October 8, 2004. Massachusetts Institute of Technology, Cambridge, MA.

Donahue, Phil. Interview by David Skover. Tape recording, September 20, 2010. New York City.

Gitlin, Todd. Interview by David Skover. Tape recording, July 19, 2004. Columbia University, New York City.

Green, Steven K. Interview by David Skover. Tape recording, January 8, 2011. Willamette University School of Law, Salem, OR.

Greenawalt, Kent. Interview by David Skover. Tape recording, July 20, 2004. Columbia University, New York City.

Jansen, Sue Curry. Interview by David Skover. Tape recording, August 25, 2010. Muhlenberg College, Allentown, PA.

Jhally, Sut. Interview by David Skover. Tape recording, August 12, 2010. University of Massachusetts at Amherst, Amherst, MA.

Krug, Anita K. Interview by Ronald Collins and David Skover. Tape recording, May 12, 2012. University of Washington School of Law, Seattle, WA.

Linde, Hans A. Interview by David Skover. Tape recording, February 14, 2004. Willamette University School of Law, Salem, OR.

MacKinnon, Catharine A. Interview by David Skover. Tape recording, May 17, 2004. University of Chicago School of Law, Chicago, IL.

Nader, Ralph. Interview by Ronald Collins and David Skover. Tape recording, September 16, 2010. Center of Study for Responsive Law, Washington, DC.

Newman, Judge Jon O. Interview by David Skover. Tape recording, January 26, 2011. Sarasota, FL.

Nussbaum, Martha C. Interview by David Skover. Tape recording, January 18, 2011. University of Chicago School of Law, Chicago, IL.

Schauer, Frederick. Interview by David Skover. Tape recording, October 11, 2004. Harvard University School of Law, Cambridge, MA.

Shiffrin, Steven. Interview by David Skover. Tape recording, August 27, 2010. Cornell University School of Law, Ithaca, NY.

Stevelman, Faith. Interview by Ronald Collins and David Skover. Tape recording, April 15, 2012. Seattle University School of Law, Seattle, WA.

Stone, Geoffrey. Interview by David Skover. Tape recording, May 17, 2004. University of Chicago School of Law, Chicago, IL.

Strossen, Nadine. Interview by David Skover. Tape recording, September 21, 2010. New York Law School, New York City.

Walzer, Michael. Interview by David Skover. Tape recording, September 20, 2010. New York University, New York City.

West, Cornel. Interview by David Skover. Tape recording, September 22, 2010. Princeton University, Princeton, NJ.

Zinn, Howard. Interview by David Skover. Tape recording, October 11, 2004. Boston University, Boston, MA.

Among the most prominent books that bear strong *theoretical connections* to our general theses in *On Dissent* are the following:

Carter, Stephen L. *The Dissent of the Governed: A Meditation on Law, Religion, and Loyalty*. Cambridge, MA: Harvard University Press, 1998. (Describing the legitimacy of the state as measured by its dissenters' tolerance for authority.)

Commager, Henry Steele. *Freedom, Loyalty, Dissent*. New York: Oxford University Press, 1954. (Recognizing that American history was rooted in dissent, and that we encourage it because a healthy state cannot live without it.)

Euchner, Charles C. *Extraordinary Politics: How Protest and Dissent Are Changing American Democracy*. Boulder, CO: Westview Press, 1996. (With an eye to the dynamics of "ordinary politics," an exploration of dissent and protest as forms of "extraordinary politics.")

Fortas, Abe. *Concerning Dissent and Civil Disobedience*. New York: Signet Books, 1968. (Focusing on the contours of the right to dissent and offering classic cases of civil disobedience as examples of rightful dissent.)

Gitlin, Todd. *The Intellectuals and the Flag*. New York: Columbia University Press, 2006. (Examining popular culture as a surrogate for political action.)

Lovell, Jarret S. *Crimes of Dissent: Civil Disobedience, Criminal Justice, and the Politics of Conscience*. New York: New York University Press, 2009. (Detailing the actions of "criminals" who deliberately and publicly violate the law as expressions of protest against perceived racial, economic, or other social injustices.)

Penalver, Eduardo Moises and Sonia K. Katyal. *Property Outlaws: How Squatters, Pirates, and Protesters Improve the Law of Ownership*. New Haven, CT: Yale University Press, 2010. (Drawing attention to the general question of change within real and intellectual property rights and the crucial function played by criminal and civil disobedience within that process.)

Shiffrin, Steven. *Dissent, Injustice, and the Meanings of America*. Princeton, NJ: Princeton University Press, 2000. (Positing that dissenters stand at the center of the First Amendment, and not at its periphery.)

Sunstein, Cass R. *Why Societies Need Dissent*. Cambridge, MA: Harvard University Press, 2003. (Legitimating dissent as a necessary counterforce to the destabilizing and dysfunctional social consequences of conformity; more a study of the phenomenon of conformity in its various guises and operations than a study of the phenomenon of dissent per se.)

Walzer, Michael. *The Company of Critics*. New York: Basic Books, 2002. (Arguing that criticism is most properly the work of "insiders," men and women mindful of and committed to the people whose practices and policies they call into question.)

Among the articles that focus on *specific forms of dissent*, and thus have relevance to particular dimensions of our work, are the following:

Bay, Christian. "Civil Disobedience: The Inner and Outer Limits." In *Dissent and the State*, edited by C. E. S. Franks, 40–59. Toronto: Oxford University Press, 1989. (Exploring the parameters of civil disobedience as a phenomenon.)

Berlant, Lauren. "The Epistemology of State Emotion." In *Dissent in Dangerous Times*, edited by Austin Sarat, 46–78. Ann Arbor: University of Michigan Press, 2005. (Explaining that the contemporary "war on terrorism" capitalizes on the emotionality of public rhetoric to normalize a collective response that abhors "nuanced" dissent.)

Blumer, Herbert. "Social Movements." In *The Sociology of Dissent*, edited by R. Serge Denisoff, 4–20. New York: Harcourt Brace Jovanovich, 1974. (Contrasting "reform" with "revolution," and discussing "expressive movements," such as fashion and lifestyle choices.)

Bosmajian, Haig A. "Introduction." In *Dissent: Symbolic Behavior and Rhetorical Strategies*, edited by Haig A. Bosmajian, 1-11. Boston, MA: Allyn and Bacon, 1972. (Studying symbolic behavior as the strategy of dissenters.)

Brown, Wendy. "Political Idealization and Its Discontents." In *Dissent in Dangerous Times*, edited by Austin Sarat, 23–45. Ann Arbor: University of Michigan Press, 2005. (Exploring political love, fealty and critique through a consideration of love and idealization.)

Cheney, George and Daniel J. Lair. "Elevating Dissent and Transcending Fear-Based Culture at War and at Work." In *Dissent and the Failure of Leadership*, edited by Stephen P. Banks, 182–207. Northampton, MA: Edward Elgar Publishing, 2008. (Exploring contemporary fear in entertainment views outside mainstream positions.)

Clark, Ramsey. "The First Amendment and the Politics of Confrontation." In *Dissent, Power, and Confrontation*, edited by Alexander Klein, 3–31. New York: McGraw Hill Book Co., 1971

Corbett, Edward P. J. "The Rhetoric of the Open Hand and the Rhetoric of the Closed Fist." In *Dissent: Symbolic Behavior and Rhetorical Strategies*, edited by Haig A. Bosmaijan, 71–83. Boston, MA: Allyn and Bacon, 1972. (Analyzing the characteristics of "open hand" versus "closed fist" dissent.)

Cromley, Brent R. "The Right to Dissent in a Free Society." *Montana Law Review* 32 (1971): 215–226. (Describing the tension between a "free society" that suggests the tolerance of a right of dissent and a "system of laws" that presupposes no right to disobey the law.)

Gerken, Heather K. "Dissenting by Deciding." *Stanford Law Review* 47 (2005): 1745–1785. (Describing the phenomenon whereby those who hold a minority view within the culture as a whole enjoy majoritarian power within a local constituency.)

Grace, Elizabeth and Colin Leys. "The Concept of Subversion and Its Implications." In *Dissent and the State*, edited by C. E. S. Franks, 62–85. Toronto: Oxford University Press, 1989. (Exploring the origins and modern understanding of "subversion.")

Gusterson, Hugh. "The Weakest Link? Academic Dissent in the 'War on Terrorism.'" In *Dissent in Dangerous Times*, edited by Austin Sarat, 81–110. Ann Arbor: University of Michigan Press,

2005. (Attempts to constrict academic critics of governmental policy typically failed, because such dissent was largely ineffectual.)

Hackett, Robert A. "Dissent May Not Need to Be Disciplined: Corporate Influence in the News Media." In *Disciplining Dissent*, edited by William Bruneau and James L. Turk, 143–161. Toronto: James Lorimer and Company, 2004. (Arguing that dissent does not need to be disciplined, because mass media's institutional procedures and socialization preempt such expression in the first place.)

Horowitz, Irving Louis and Martin Liebowitz. "Social Deviance and Political Marginality." In *The Sociology of Dissent*, edited by R. Serge Denisoff, 263–280. New York: Harcourt Brace Jovanovich, 1974. (Differentiating political dissent from personal deviancy.)

Ibsen, Henrik. "Introduction." In *Protest: Man against Society*, edited by Gregory Armstrong, 15–91. New York: Bantam Books, 1969. (Examining the function of mass protest in American democratic system, and arguing that there is a duty of the citizen to protest.)

Koffler, Judith Schenck and Bennett L. Gershman. "The New Seditious Libel." *Cornell Law Review* 69 (1984): 816–882. (Tracking the history of seditious libel in Anglo-American law and analyzing our current "national state of insecurity.")

Martin, Brian. "Varieties of Dissent." In *Dissent and the Failure of Leadership*, edited by Stephen P. Banks, 22–36. Northampton, MA: Edward Elgar Publishing, 2008. (Analyzing the distinctions among disagreement, dissent, rebellion, and heresy.)

Quigley, William P. "The Necessity Defense in Civil Disobedience Cases: Bring In the Jury." *New England Law Review* 38 (2003): 3–72. (In the context of civil disobedience jury trials, it is troubling if the court refuses to permit the necessity defense to be made in cases of indirect civil disobedience.)

Rubin, Edward L. "John Newman's Theory of Disparagement and the First Amendment in the Administrative State." *New York Law Review* 46 (2002–2003): 249–277. (Suggesting that the flaccid state of dissent in modern America is partially a result of the structure and organization of the modern administrative state and the character of contemporary mass media.)

Rush, Gary B. "Toward a Definition of the Extreme Right." In *The Sociology of Dissent*, edited by R. Serge Denisoff, 210–225. New York: Harcourt Brace Jovanovich, 1974. (According dissenter status to the ideology and practices of the "extreme right" in contemporary America.)

Sarat, Austin. "Terrorism, Dissent, and Repression: An Introduction." In *Dissent in Dangerous Times*, edited by Austin Sarat, 1–19. Ann Arbor: University of Michigan Press, 2005. (Characterizing dissent during the current "war on terrorism" and the dangers of dissent during wartime.)

Sawicki, Nadia N. "The Hollow Promise of Freedom of Conscience." *Cardozo Law Review* 33 (2012): 1389–1449. (Examining the contexts in which conscience intersects most often with law – religious claims, refusals by medical providers, and military objections, among others – and arguing that U.S. law does not demonstrate respect for the theory of freedom of conscience as a general matter.)

Schauer, Frederick. "The Boundaries of the First Amendment: A Preliminary Exploration of Constitutional Salience." *Harvard Law Review* 117 (2004): 1765–1809. (Explaining America's obsession with freedoms of speech as a function, in part, of the magnetism of events of dissent and protest.)

Sunder, Madhavi. "Cultural Dissent." *Stanford Law Review* 54 (2001): 495–567. (Describing an approach to cultural conflict that recognizes "cultural dissent" within contemporary culture.)

Theoharis, Athan G. "The FBI and Dissent in the United States." In *Dissent and the State*, edited by C. E. S. Franks, 86–110. Toronto: Oxford University Press, 1989. (Examining the history of the FBI from the Roosevelt to Reagan administrations and its investigations of leftist dissenters.)

Toscano, Paul. "The Sanctity of Dissent." In *Dissent and the Failure of Leadership*, edited by Stephen P. Banks, 169–181. Northampton, MA: Edward Elgar Publishing, 2008. (Providing ten reasons for viewing dissent as a "holy" act.)

Among the most major of the *historical treatises* that describe the tradition of dissent in world cultures and in our own society are the following:

Bleiker, Roland. *Popular Dissent, Human Agency and Global Politics.* New York: Cambridge University Press, 2000.

Chang, Nancy. *Silencing Political Dissent: How Post-September 11 Anti-Terrorism Measures Threaten Our Civil Liberties.* New York: Seven Stories Press, 2002.

Cohen, Alfred E. *Minerva's Progress: Tradition and Dissent in American Culture.* New York: Harcourt Brace & World, 1946, reissued 1969.

Dunbar, Anthony, ed. *Where We Stand: Voices of Southern Dissent.* Montgomery, AL: NewSouth Books, 2004.

Dunham, Barrows. *Heroes and Heretics.* New York: Alfred A. Knopf, 1964.

Gaustad, Edwin Scott. *Dissent in American Religion.* Chicago: University of Chicago Press, rev. ed. 2006.

Green, Steven K. *The Second Disestablishment: Church and State in Nineteenth Century America.* New York: Oxford University Press, 2010.

Hamilton, Neil. *Rebels and Renegades.* New York: Routledge, 2002.

Hecht, Jennifer Michael. *Doubt: A History.* San Francisco: Harper, 2003.

Howe, Irving, ed. *Twenty-Five Years of Dissent: An American Tradition.* New York: Methuen, 1979.

Ivie, Robert L. *Dissent from War.* Bloomfield, CT: Kumarian Press, 2007.

Jackson, Perceival E. *Dissent in the Supreme Court: A Chronology.* Norman: University of Oklahoma Press, 1969.

Kampf, Louis, ed. *Counter-Tradition: A Reader in the Literature of Dissent and Alternatives.* New York: Basic Books, 1971.

Kalven, Jr., Harry. *The Negro and the First Amendment.* Columbus: Ohio State University Press, 1965.

Klement, Frank L. *The Limits of Dissent: Clement L. Vallandigham and the Civil War.* New York: Fordham University Press, 1998.

Larsen, Ojvind. *The Right to Dissent: The Critical Principle in Discourse Ethics and Deliberative Democracy.* Copenhagen: Museum Tusculanum Press / University of Copenhagen, 2009.

Laursen, John Christian, ed. *Difference and Dissent. Theories of Toleration in Medieval and Early Modern Europe.* New York: Rowman and Littlefield, 1996.

Levi, Margaret. *Consent, Dissent, and Patriotism.* New York: Cambridge University Press, 1997.

Levy, Leonard. *Blasphemy: Verbal Offense against the Sacred, from Moses to Salman Rushdie.* New York: Alfred A. Knopf, 1993.

Lovell, Jarret S. *Crimes of Dissent: Civil Disobedience, Criminal Justice, and the Politics of Conscience.* New York: New York University Press, 2009.

Martin, Robert W. T. *Government by Dissent: Protest, Resistance, and Radical Democratic Thought in The Early American Republic.* New York: New York University Press, 2013.

Masheder, Richard. *Dissent and Democracy: Their Mutual Relations and Common Object: An Historical Review.* London: Bradbury and Evans, 1864.

Mayers, David. *Dissenting Voices in America's Rise to Power.* New York: Cambridge University Press, 2007.

Moore, R. I. *The Origins of European Dissent.* New York: St. Martin's Press, 1977.

Morison, Samuel Eliot, Frederick Merck, and Frank Freidel. *Dissent in Three American Wars.* Cambridge, MA: Harvard University Press, 1970.

Nederman, Cary J. and John Christian Laursen. *Difference and Dissent: Theories of Toleration in Medieval and Early Modern Europe.* New York: Rowman & Littlefield, 1996.

Nussbaum, Martha C. *Liberty of Conscience: In Defense of America's Tradition of Religious Equality.* New York: Basic Books, 2008.

Ober, Josiah. *Political Dissent in Democratic Athens: Intellectual Critics of Popular Rule.* Princeton, NJ: Princeton University Press, 1998.

Routley, Erik. *English Religious Dissent.* New York: Cambridge University Press, 2009.

Schultz, Bud and Ruth Schultz. *The Price of Dissent.* Berkeley: University of California Press, 2001.

Shepard, Benjamin and Ronald Hayduck. *From ACT UP to the WTO.* New York: Verso, 2002.

Stein, Stephen J. *Communities of Dissent: A History of Alternative Religions in America.* New York: Oxford University Press, 2003.

Young, Ralph E. *Dissent in America: The Voices That Shaped a Nation.* New York: Pearson Education, 2006.

Zick, Timothy. *Speech Out of Doors: Preserving First Amendment Liberties in Public Places.* New York: Cambridge University Press, 2009.

INDEX